Blackstone's
Police Q&A

General Police Duties 2020

Blackstone's
Police Q&A

General Police Duties 2020

Eighteenth edition

Huw Smart and John Watson

OXFORD
UNIVERSITY PRESS

UNIVERSITY PRESS

Great Clarendon Street, Oxford, OX2 6DP,
United Kingdom

Oxford University Press is a department of the University of Oxford.
It furthers the University's objective of excellence in research, scholarship,
and education by publishing worldwide. Oxford is a registered trade mark of
Oxford University Press in the UK and in certain other countries

Published in the United States of America by Oxford University Press
198 Madison Avenue, New York, NY 10016, United States of America

British Library Cataloguing in Publication Data

Data available

ISBN 978–0–19–884870–7

Printed in Great Britain by
Bell & Bain Ltd., Glasgow

Contents

Contents

Introduction

Before you get into the detail of this book, there are two myths about multiple-choice questions (MCQs) that we need to get out of the way right at the start:

1. that they are easy to answer;
2. that they are easy to write.

Take one look at a professionally designed and properly developed exam paper such as those used by the Police Promotion Examinations Board or the National Board of Medical Examiners in the US and the first myth collapses straight away. Contrary to what some people believe, MCQs are not an easy solution for examiners and not a 'multiple-guess' soft option for examinees.

That is not to say that *all* MCQs are taxing, or even testing—in the psychometric sense. If MCQs are to have any real value at all, they need to be carefully designed and follow some agreed basic rules.

And this leads us to myth number 2.

It is widely assumed by many people and educational organisations that anyone with the knowledge of a subject can write MCQs. You need only look at how few MCQ writing courses are offered by training providers in the UK to see just how far this myth is believed. Similarly, you need only to have a go at a few badly designed MCQs to realise that it is a myth nonetheless. Writing bad MCQs is easy; writing good ones is no easier than answering them!

There are several purposes for which MCQs are very useful. The first is in producing a reliable, valid and fair test of knowledge and understanding across a wide range of subject matter. Another is an aid to study, preparation and revision for such examinations and tests. The differences in objective mean that there are slight differences in the rules that the MCQ writers follow. Whereas the design of fully validated MCQs to be used in high stakes examinations, which will effectively determine who passes and who fails, has very strict guidelines as to construction, content and style, less stringent rules apply to MCQs that are being used for teaching and revision. For that reason, there may be types of MCQ that are appropriate in the latter setting which would not be used in the former. However, in developing the MCQs for this book, the authors have tried to follow the fundamental rules of MCQ design but they would not claim to have replicated the level of psychometric rigour that is—and has to be—adopted by the type of examining bodies referred to previously.

These MCQs are designed to reinforce your knowledge and understanding, to highlight any gaps or weaknesses in that knowledge and understanding, and to help focus your revision of the relevant topics.

Good luck!

Blackstone's Police Q&As—Special Features

References to Blackstone's Police Manuals

Every answer is followed by a paragraph reference to Blackstone's Police Manuals. This means that once you have attempted a question and looked at an answer, the Manual can immediately be referred to for help and clarification.

Unique numbers for each question

Each question and answer has the same unique number. This should ensure that there is no confusion as to which question is linked to which answer. For example, Question 2.1 is linked to Answer 2.1.

Checklists

The checklists are designed to help you keep track of your progress when answering the multiple-choice questions. If you fill in the checklist after attempting a question, you will be able to check how many you got right on the first attempt and will know immediately which questions need to be revisited a second time. Please visit www.blackstonespoliceservice.com and click through to the Blackstone's Police Q&As 2020 page. You will then find electronic versions of the checklists to download and print out. Email any queries or comments on the book to: police.uk@oup.com.

Acknowledgements

This book has been written as an accompaniment to Blackstone's Police Manuals, and will test the knowledge you have accrued through reading that series. It is of the essence that full study of the relevant chapters in each Police Manual is completed prior to attempting the Questions and Answers. As qualified police trainers we recognise that students tend to answer questions incorrectly either because they don't read the question properly, or because one of the 'distracters' has done its work. The distracter is one of the three incorrect answers in a multiple-choice question (MCQ), and is designed to distract you from the correct answer and in this way discriminate between candidates: the better-prepared candidate not being 'distracted'.

So particular attention should be paid to the *Answers* sections, and students should ask themselves 'Why did I get that question wrong?' and, just as importantly, 'Why did I get that question right?' Combining the information gained in the *Answers* section together with rereading the chapter in the Police Manuals should lead to greater understanding of the subject matter.

The authors wish to thank all the staff at Oxford University Press who have helped put this publication together.

1 | Complaints and Misconduct

STUDY PREPARATION

The maintenance of proper professional standards is paramount to all police officers, supervisors and managers—and the communities they serve.

The chapter guides you through the misconduct procedures, including the effect on individual officers and line managers, and misconduct meetings, tribunals, appeals and suspension from duties.

The Independent Office for Police Conduct (IOPC) has an oversight role in complaints against police officers, whether by supervising, managing or independently investigating a matter.

QUESTIONS

Question 1.1

Assistant Chief Constable MOREL was on suspension from duty, having been accused of a criminal offence under s. 2 of the Computer Misuse Act 1990. The officer was being investigated for accessing and using confidential information from a police computer system. Whilst on suspension, Assistant Chief Constable MOREL gave an interview to a national newspaper, claiming to be innocent and that he was being harassed by the force investigating the incident.

Could Assistant Chief Constable MOREL have breached the Standards of Professional Behaviour, under the Police (Conduct) Regulations 2012 (Discreditable Conduct), by giving the interview to the press?

A No, the Regulations only apply to police officers up to and including the rank of chief superintendent.

B Yes, the Regulations apply to all police officers, up to and including the rank of assistant chief constable.

C No, the Regulations do not apply to police officers who are suspended, regardless of their rank.

D Yes, the Regulations apply to all police officers, whether they are suspended or not.

Question 1.2

Constable GOULDING is in police detention for providing a positive breath test, having been involved in a fail to stop road traffic collision whilst off duty. The officer in the case intends interviewing Constable GOULDING, who is represented by the duty solicitor.

Is Constable GOULDING also entitled to have a police 'friend' present at the interview, in these circumstances?

A No, a police 'friend' may not be present at an interview in connection with a criminal offence which was committed off duty.

B Yes, Constable GOULDING would be entitled to have a police 'friend' present at the interview, as well as the solicitor.

C No, a police 'friend' may not be present at an interview in connection with a criminal offence.

D No, a police 'friend' may not be present at an interview in connection with a criminal offence, committed whilst off duty, when the offence is not connected to the person's role as a police officer.

Question 1.3

Constable KEMP has been charged with causing the death of a pedestrian by dangerous driving—the officer was pursuing a stolen vehicle at the time of the incident and was not trained to do so. The Independent Office for Police Conduct (IOPC) has decided to independently investigate the incident. Constable KEMP's force (the appropriate authority) is considering whether or not the officer should be suspended from duty.

Which of the following statements is correct, as to the role the IOPC should play in the decision as to whether Constable KEMP should be suspended?

A If the IOPC is independently investigating a matter, it has decision-making powers as to whether police officers should be suspended.

B If it is independently investigating a matter, the appropriate authority should consult with the IOPC, but the decision rests with the force.

C If it is supervising, managing or independently investigating a matter, the appropriate authority should consult with the IOPC, but the decision rests with the force.

D If the IOPC is supervising, managing or independently investigating a matter, it has decision-making powers as to whether police officers should be suspended.

Question 1.4

Constable MURPHY is being investigated for a misconduct matter, but is currently on certificated sick leave, having had a back operation. The officer is not expected to return to work for several months; however, the investigating officer is keen to progress the complaint as soon as possible and wishes to interview Constable MURPHY. The officer's Police Federation representative has emailed the investigating officer, claiming it would be unfair to conduct an interview while the member is on sick leave.

Which of the following is correct, in relation to whether an interview could be conducted while Constable MURPHY is on sick leave?

A Constable MURPHY may be interviewed or alternatively, the investigating officer may send questions to the officer, requesting a written response.

B Police officers may be interviewed while on certified sick leave, if the allegation against them is considered to be serious enough.

C Police officers may not be interviewed while on certified sick leave; this would amount to a breach of the Conduct Regulations.

D Constable MURPHY may be interviewed while on certified sick leave, but the interview must be conducted in person.

Question 1.5

Sergeant VAUGHAN has been asked to attend a misconduct meeting, following a Professional Standards Department investigation into a complaint from a member of the public. The allegation was that Sergeant VAUGHAN swore at the complainant, who was reporting an incident at the station. Sergeant VAUGHAN intends denying the incident and has asked for the station enquiry clerk, who was present during the incident, to attend the meeting as a witness. The investigating officer, on the other hand, has identified an independent member of the public, who was present at the time, and who is prepared to attend as a witness.

Which of the following statements is correct, in respect of witnesses attending misconduct meetings?

A Because Sergeant VAUGHAN has asked for a witness to attend, the person conducting the meeting must ask the station enquiry clerk to attend.

B The person conducting the meeting is only entitled to ask the independent witness identified by the Professional Standards Department to attend.

C The person conducting the meeting will decide if witnesses are required, depending on whether or not their attendance is necessary to resolve disputed issues in the case.

D Neither person should be asked to attend; witnesses are only allowed to give evidence in misconduct hearings.

Question 1.6

Constable WOODS is attending a misconduct hearing, having been accused of passing information to a member of the public, which was stored on the force intelligence system. The officer is accused of breaching the 'Confidentiality' standard included in the ten Standards of Professional Behaviour.

Which of the following is correct, in relation to who should hear the misconduct matter, in these circumstances?

A It should be heard by a panel, which may be chaired by a senior police officer.

B It should be heard by a panel, which must be chaired by a legally qualified person.

C It should be heard by a panel, which may be chaired either by a legally qualified person, or a senior human resources professional with sufficient seniority.

D It should be heard by a panel, which may be chaired either by a senior police officer, or a senior human resources professional with sufficient seniority.

Question 1.7

The Independent Office for Police Conduct (IOPC) has conducted a managed investigation into an allegation of misconduct against Constable KELLY and the officer has been given notification to attend a misconduct hearing. Constable ATKINS has attended a meeting with a Police Federation representative and is concerned that the hearing may be held in public.

Which of the following statements is correct in relation to this issue?

A The hearing may be held in public if the IOPC considers that because of its gravity or other exceptional circumstances it is in the public interest to do so.

B The hearing may not be held in public because the IOPC did not conduct an independent investigation into the allegation.

C The hearing may be held in public if the appropriate authority considers it is in the public interest to do so.

D The hearing may be held in public, but only if this is a case that could lead to Constable KELLY's dismissal.

Question 1.8

Constable HURLEY has been given notification to attend a misconduct hearing, having been convicted of a criminal offence in a domestic-related incident. An independent investigation has been conducted by the Independent Office for Police Conduct (IOPC) and it is considering whether or not to direct that the misconduct hearing should be held in public.

If the misconduct hearing is to be held in public, is the IOPC required to consult with anyone beforehand?

A Yes, with the appropriate authority, Constable HURLEY, the complainant and any witnesses.

B Yes, with the complainant only.

C No, the IOPC may make this direction regardless of any consultation.

D Yes, with the appropriate authority, the complainant and any witnesses.

Question 1.9

Constable DAWSON is attending a misconduct meeting, having been accused of being abusive towards the complainant, FROST, during a routine road traffic check. FROST has been asked by the officer conducting the meeting to attend to give evidence of Constable DAWSON's behaviour.

Which of the following statements is correct in respect of FROST's attendance at the meeting?

A FROST must leave the meeting immediately after giving evidence.

B Because this is a misconduct meeting and not a hearing, FROST may remain for the entire proceedings.

C FROST must leave the meeting once the officer conducting it has made a finding.

D FROST may remain at the meeting after giving evidence, but must leave after any character reference/mitigation is given, before the outcome is decided.

Question 1.10

Assistant Chief Constable WALL has attended a misconduct meeting with the deputy chief constable. Assistant Chief Constable WALL was given a written warning at the meeting and is now seeking legal advice about making an appeal against the finding to a Police Appeals Tribunal.

Is Assistant Chief Constable WALL entitled to make such an appeal in these circumstances?

A No, the Police Appeals Tribunal does not hear appeals against the findings or outcomes of a misconduct meeting.
B Yes, an appeal may be made to a Police Appeals Tribunal against any misconduct finding.
C Yes, an appeal may be made by an assistant chief constable against the finding or outcome of a misconduct meeting.
D No, the Police Appeals Tribunal only hears appeals against the findings or outcomes of a special case hearing for gross misconduct.

Question 1.11

PC OWEN's abusive behaviour towards several members of the public has been cause for complaint. The assessment of PC OWEN's behaviour determined that he did not meet the Standards of Professional Behaviour and this eventually led to a misconduct meeting. At the misconduct meeting, PC OWEN was given a written warning regarding his behaviour and was told that the written warning will be put on his personal file.

For how long will that written warning remain 'live' on PC OWEN's file?

A Six months from the date the warning was given.
B 12 months from the date the warning was given.
C 18 months from the date the warning was given.
D 24 months from the date the warning was given.

ANSWERS

Answer 1.1

Answer **D** — The Police (Conduct) Regulations 2012 are supported by a code of ethics—the Standards of Professional Behaviour. The Standards apply to police officers of *all* ranks from chief constable to constable (including special constables). Answers A and B are therefore incorrect. (If you answered A to this question, you may have been considering the Police (Performance) Regulations 2012, which only apply to police officers (including special constables) up to and including the rank of chief superintendent.)

The Standards of Professional Behaviour do apply to police officers who are subject to suspension; therefore, answer C is incorrect.

General Police Duties, para. 4.1.1

Answer 1.2

Answer **D** — A police officer has a right to be accompanied by a police 'friend' at all stages of any misconduct proceedings (under the Police (Conduct) Regulations 2012). This includes interviews, misconduct meetings and hearings.

A police officer is also entitled, in certain circumstances, to be accompanied by a police 'friend' at an interview in connection with a criminal offence. Therefore, answer C is incorrect.

However, the circumstances in which a police officer is entitled to be accompanied by a police 'friend' at an interview in connection with a criminal offence are very narrow. If the officer is arrested or interviewed in connection with a criminal offence committed whilst off duty *that has no connection with his/her role as a serving police officer*, then the police 'friend' has no right to attend the criminal interview of that police officer. Answers A and B are incorrect for this reason.

General Police Duties, para. 4.1.3

Answer 1.3

Answer **C** — In cases where the IOPC is supervising, managing or independently investigating a matter, the appropriate authority will consult with the IOPC before making a decision whether to suspend or not. Answer B is incorrect, as this requirement applies whether the IOPC is supervising, managing or independently investigating a matter.

However, whatever the role the IOPC plays in the investigation, it is the appropriate authority's decision whether to suspend a police officer or not. Answers A and D are therefore incorrect.

Note that the appropriate authority must also consult the IOPC before making the decision to allow a police officer to resume his/her duties following suspension (unless the suspension ends because there will be no misconduct or special case proceedings or because these have concluded) in cases where the IOPC is supervising, managing or independently investigating a case involving that police officer.

General Police Duties, para. 4.1.5.1

Answer 1.4

Answer **A** — Where a police officer is on certificated sick leave, the investigator should seek to establish when the police officer will be fit for interview. It may be that the police officer is not fit for ordinary police duty but is perfectly capable of being interviewed. This is regardless of how serious the allegation is and answers B and C are incorrect.

Alternatively the police officer concerned *may* be invited to provide a written response to the allegations within a specified period and *may* be sent the questions that the investigator wishes to be answered. Answer D is therefore incorrect.

General Police Duties, para. 4.1.5.5

Answer 1.5

Answer **C** — Generally speaking, misconduct meetings and hearings will be conducted without witnesses. A witness *may* be required to attend a misconduct meeting or hearing if the person conducting or chairing the meeting/hearing reasonably believes his/her attendance is necessary to resolve disputed issues in that case. Answer D is incorrect, as witnesses *may* be asked to attend meetings *or* hearings.

The officer concerned *may* ask for witnesses to attend; however, it will be for the person conducting the meeting or hearing to decide whether to allow such witnesses, if their attendance is necessary to resolve any disputed issues in the case. On the other hand, the person conducting the meeting or hearing may decide not to have any witnesses at the meeting/hearing. Answers A and B are incorrect, because either witness could have been asked to attend, but the decision will be made by the person conducting the meeting or hearing.

General Police Duties, para. 4.1.5.9

Answer 1.6

Answer **B** — A misconduct *meeting* for non-senior officers (police officers up to and including the rank of chief superintendent and all special constables) will be heard by a police officer (or other member of a police force) of at least one rank above the police officer concerned.

However, the officer in this case has been invited to a misconduct *hearing*. A misconduct hearing for non-senior officers will consist of a three-person panel. The chair will always be a *legally qualified person*.

Answers A, C and D are therefore incorrect.

General Police Duties, para. 4.1.6.3

Answer 1.7

Answer **B** — Where a misconduct hearing (not misconduct meetings) arises from a case where the IOPC has conducted an *independent* investigation (in accordance with para. 19 of sch. 3 to the 2002 Act) and the IOPC considers that because of its gravity or other exceptional circumstances it would be in the public interest to do so, the IOPC may, having consulted with the appropriate authority, the police officer concerned, the complainant and any witnesses, direct that the whole or part of the misconduct hearing will be held in public.

Since this was a managed investigation, and not an independent investigation, it does not fall within the criteria for the hearing to be held in public and answers A, C and D are incorrect.

General Police Duties, para. 4.1.6.4

Answer 1.8

Answer **A** — Where a misconduct hearing (not misconduct meetings) arises from a case where the IOPC has conducted an independent investigation (in accordance with para. 19 of sch. 3 to the 2002 Act) and the IOPC considers that because of its gravity or other exceptional circumstances it would be in the public interest to do so, the IOPC may, having consulted with *the appropriate authority, the police officer concerned, the complainant and any witnesses*, direct that the whole or part of the misconduct hearing will be held in public.

Answers B, C and D are therefore incorrect.

General Police Duties, para. 4.1.6.4

Answer 1.9

Answer **C** — A complainant and any person accompanying the complainant will be permitted to remain in the meeting/hearing up to and including any finding by the persons conducting the meeting/hearing, after having given evidence (if appropriate). Answers A and B are therefore incorrect.

However, the complainant and any person accompanying the complainant will *not* be permitted to remain in the meeting/hearing while character references or mitigation are being given or the decision of the panel as to the outcome is being given. Answer D is incorrect, as the person must leave *before* the character reference or mitigation is given (which will also be before the outcome is given).

Note that the appropriate authority will have a duty to inform the complainant of the outcome of any misconduct meeting/hearing whether the complainant attends or not.

General Police Duties, para. 4.1.6.13

Answer 1.10

Answer **C** — A police officer has a right of appeal to a Police Appeals Tribunal against any disciplinary finding and/or disciplinary outcome imposed at a misconduct hearing or special case hearing held under the Conduct Regulations. Senior police officers (assistant chief constables and above), in addition, have the right to appeal to a Police Appeals Tribunal against any disciplinary finding and/or outcome imposed at a misconduct meeting. Since a Police Appeals Tribunal *may* hear an appeal in relation to a finding at a misconduct meeting, answer A is incorrect.

However, since this right is restricted to senior police officers, answer B is incorrect.

Answer D is incorrect because appeals can be made against findings in misconduct hearings *or* special case hearings (or meetings in the case of an ACC).

General Police Duties, para. 4.1.9

Answer 1.11

Answer **B** — When a written warning is given, the warning will be put on the personal file of the officer concerned and will remain 'live' for a period of 12 months from the date on which the warning was given.

General Police Duties, para. 4.1.6.10

2 | Unsatisfactory Performance and Attendance

STUDY PREPARATION

The previous chapter dealt with the Police (Conduct) Regulations 2012. In this chapter, we examine the Police (Performance) Regulations 2012.

These Regulations cover both performance and absence management, and the chapter guides you through the procedures for dealing with both aspects of the regulations.

The emphasis is on improving poor performance and attendance, instead of punishing individuals. As a line manager, you will find that the aspects of misconduct and performance are closely related.

The final part of this chapter deals with the offences that can be committed by people in public offices, including police officers, who abuse their powers.

QUESTIONS

Question 2.1

Sergeant KHAN has been concerned about the attendance record of Constable HEALD and has asked the officer to attend a meeting to discuss the matter. It has been decided that the issue will be dealt with by management action, rather than the unsatisfactory performance procedures. Constable HEALD admitted that her attendance could be better and has agreed to submit to an action plan to be set by Sergeant KHAN.

Which of the following statements is correct regarding the period of time Sergeant KHAN should set, to allow an improvement in attendance by Constable HEALD?

A Because the matter is being dealt with by management action, an automatic period of three months should be set.

B Because the matter relates to attendance, an automatic period of three months should be set.

C Because the matter is being dealt with by management action, there is no limit to the period of time that may be set.

D There is no set period; however, Sergeant KHAN should allow sufficient time to provide a reasonable opportunity for Constable HEALD to improve attendance.

Question 2.2

Sergeant GREEGAN is due to hold a first stage unsatisfactory performance meeting with Constable O'NEIL in an hour's time, regarding the continued submission of poor paperwork. Sergeant GREEGAN has also been concerned with Constable O'NEIL's poor timekeeping and has recently had to warn the officer several times for arriving at work late. Sergeant GREEGAN is considering discussing the additional matter at the first stage meeting, alongside the original unsatisfactory performance matter.

How should Sergeant GREEGAN proceed in these circumstances?

A The planned meeting should continue and a separate first stage meeting should be arranged to discuss the additional matter. Unconnected unsatisfactory performance matters must always be dealt with separately.

B Sergeant GREEGAN may adjourn the planned meeting and arrange a first stage meeting at a later date to discuss both matters.

C Sergeant GREEGAN may discuss both matters at the planned meeting, because new information has come to light about Constable O'NEIL's performance during the specified period.

D The planned meeting should continue and a separate first stage meeting should be arranged to discuss the additional matter. Matters may only be consolidated if a person reaches stage three of the unsatisfactory performance procedures.

Question 2.3

Sergeant GANT has arranged a first stage unsatisfactory performance meeting with Constable RUSH to discuss the officer's poor attendance record. Sergeant GANT intends issuing the officer with an improvement notice, seeking an improvement in the officer's attendance at work. Sergeant GANT is newly promoted and wishes to seek advice on how to conduct the meeting and the possible outcomes.

Which of the following statements is correct, in relation to the advice Sergeant GANT may seek?

A Sergeant GANT may ask a human resources professional to be present, or a police officer with relevant experience, who is independent of the line management chain.

B Sergeant GANT may seek advice from a human resources professional, or a police officer with relevant experience, before the meeting, but they may not be present.

C Because the meeting is to do with attendance and not performance, Sergeant GANT must have a human resources professional present.

D Sergeant GANT may ask a human resources professional to be present, or a police officer who is part of the line management chain, provided the officer is not the second line manager.

Question 2.4

Constable CROSS has been asked to attend a first stage unsatisfactory performance meeting to discuss the officer's poor performance. Before the meeting, Constable CROSS met with Constable BECK, a Police Federation representative. They were discussing whether or not Constable BECK should make any representations on behalf of Constable CROSS in relation to the matter.

Which of the following statements is correct regarding any representations that either Constable CROSS or Constable BECK may make?

A Because this is a first stage unsatisfactory performance meeting, Constable BECK may not attend, but may submit written representations beforehand; Constable CROSS may make verbal representations at the meeting.

B Constable BECK may attend, but must submit written representations at the meeting; Constable CROSS may make verbal representations at the meeting.

C Because this is a first stage unsatisfactory performance meeting, Constable BECK may not attend and is not entitled to make representations; Constable CROSS may make written or verbal representations at the meeting.

D Constable BECK may attend and either she or Constable CROSS may make written or verbal representations at the meeting.

Question 2.5

Constable DALE attended an unsatisfactory performance meeting with her line manager, Sergeant MALIK. The officer had previously been given a written improvement notice at a first stage meeting, relating to her paperwork submission, and was subject to a three-month action plan. Sergeant MALIK considered that her performance had not improved in that period. At the meeting, Constable DALE asked her sergeant if there was any way her action plan could be extended, rather than proceeding to the next stage.

Would Sergeant MALIK be in a position to agree to the request to extend the improvement period?

A Yes, for up to three months, unless there are exceptional reasons for extending the period beyond six months in total.

B Yes, for up to six months, unless there are exceptional reasons for extending the period beyond nine months in total.

C Yes, for up to nine months, but the period must not exceed 12 months in total.

D Yes, for up to nine months, unless there are exceptional reasons for extending the period beyond 12 months in total.

Question 2.6

Constable POUNDS has been subject to a three-month action plan for poor attendance, following the issue of an improvement notice at a first stage unsatisfactory performance meeting. Constable POUNDS has not reported sick during this period and is now meeting Sergeant HALES to discuss the next steps. Sergeant HALES has informed the officer he needs to maintain attendance during the 'validity period' now that the current action plan has been achieved.

Which of the following statements is correct, in relation to the 'validity period' during which Constable POUNDS has to maintain attendance?

A Constable POUNDS has to maintain attendance for another three months to avoid moving to the next stage.

B Constable POUNDS has to maintain attendance for another six months to avoid moving to the next stage.

C Constable POUNDS has to maintain attendance for another nine months to avoid moving to the next stage.

D Constable POUNDS has to maintain attendance for another 12 months to avoid moving to the next stage.

Question 2.7

Detective Sergeant HUTTON is under investigation for failing to investigate a suspicious sudden death correctly. The officer was called to the scene and missed several basic investigative opportunities which, had they been recognised at the time, would have led the police to conclude that the deceased had been murdered. During the inquiry, the Professional Standards Department interviewed Detective Sergeant HUTTON's line manager, Detective Inspector PURDY, who disclosed that she had been gathering negative evidence relating to the officer's performance and attendance, with a view to placing Detective Sergeant HUTTON on an action plan. The investigating officer concluded that Detective Sergeant HUTTON's investigation of the sudden death was 'grossly incompetent'.

The Police (Performance) Regulations 2012 allow for procedures to be initiated immediately at the third stage, when an officer is deemed to be 'grossly incompetent'. In respect of these Regulations, which of the following statements is correct?

A The appropriate authority may take into account the current investigative failures, as well as any other similar, recent performance matters, when deciding whether or not procedures should be initiated immediately at the third stage.

B The appropriate authority may only initiate procedures at the third stage immediately in respect of a single incident, which could include the investigative failures at the sudden death.

C The appropriate authority may take into account the current investigative failures, as well as any other recent performance or attendance matters, when deciding whether or not procedures should be initiated immediately at the third stage.

D The appropriate authority should take into account the current investigative failures, any recent performance matters and any other acts over a period of time, when deciding whether or not procedures should be initiated immediately at the third stage.

Question 2.8

A meeting is being held between Inspector HAKES and JENNINGS, a human resources adviser, regarding the performance of Special Constable ANDERSON who works on the inspector's team. Special Constable ANDERSON is currently at the second stage of the unsatisfactory performance procedures and has recently failed an action plan. Inspector HAKES is seeking advice on what should happen next and whether it is appropriate for the officer to progress to the third stage of the procedures.

Which of the following statements is correct in relation to special constables and third stage meetings?

A Because special constables are unpaid volunteers, it is inappropriate for Special Constable ANDERSON to attend a third stage meeting.

B Special Constable ANDERSON may be required to attend a third stage meeting, but a senior special constable will be appointed to attend the meeting to advise her.

C Special Constable ANDERSON may be required to attend a third stage meeting, but a senior special constable will be appointed to attend the meeting to advise the panel.

D Special Constable ANDERSON may be required to attend a third stage meeting, but a senior special constable will be appointed to attend the meeting to form part of the panel.

Question 2.9

Constable PARKER has been on sick leave for 11 months having suffered a broken leg playing football. The officer has had two operations and is still unfit to return to work. Constable PARKER is currently at the second stage of the unsatisfactory performance procedures and has failed an action plan which required him to return to work. Consideration is being given to serving Constable PARKER with a notice to attend a stage three meeting; however, the officer's Police Federation representative has stated that he is unfit for duty, which renders him unable to attend a meeting, quoting the provisions of reg. 33 of the Police Regulations 2003 (sick leave).

What impact does Constable PARKER's injury have on the panel being able to require him to attend the meeting?

A The Regulations do not apply; Constable PARKER may be unfit for duty, but he must attend the meeting.

B The Regulations will apply; when a constable is unfit for duty, he/she will also be unfit to attend a meeting.

C When an officer is incapacitated, the meeting must be deferred until he/she is sufficiently improved to attend.

D The Regulations do not apply; the meeting may be held at a location convenient to Constable PARKER, or if necessary, in the officer's absence.

Question 2.10

Sergeant LORING was approached by Special Constable MALLET who was concerned about the behaviour of HEBDON who had recently resigned as a special constable. Special Constable MALLET told the sergeant that before he resigned, HEBDON falsely claimed to

2. Unsatisfactory Performance and Attendance

have lost his warrant card and obtained a duplicate. HEBDON had recently been overheard in a pub boasting that he had a police warrant card that he could use to get favours.

If HEBDON is in possession of a warrant card in these circumstances, which of the following is correct in relation to offences under the Police Act 1996?

A HEBDON is guilty of impersonation, because of his possession of the warrant card.

B HEBDON cannot be guilty of an offence under this Act because he is not in possession of a police uniform.

C HEBDON cannot be guilty of an offence under this Act unless evidence is available that he has used the warrant card to impersonate a police officer.

D HEBDON may be guilty of an offence under this Act because he does not have possession of the warrant card for a lawful purpose.

ANSWERS

Answer 2.1

Answer **D** — Management action should be used when a line manager identifies performance or attendance failures at an early stage. It provides an opportunity for the supervisor to discuss any improvement required, before progressing to the more formal unsatisfactory performance procedures. Ideally performance or attendance will improve and continue to an acceptable level and where there is insufficient or unsustained improvement, it will then be appropriate to use the unsatisfactory performance procedures.

There is no set period of time for an action plan at this stage, whether the line manager is dealing with a performance or attendance failure (answers A and B are therefore incorrect). The length of the plan agreed or determined by the line manager must be *sufficient to provide a reasonable opportunity for the desired improvement or attendance to take place*. The period may not be unlimited; therefore, Answer C is incorrect.

General Police Duties, para. 4.2.5

Answer 2.2

Answer **B** — Generally, a police officer can only move to a later stage of the unsatisfactory performance procedures in relation to unsatisfactory performance or attendance that is similar to, or connected with, the performance or attendance referred to in any previous written improvement notice. Where failings relate to different forms of unsatisfactory performance or attendance it will be necessary to commence each unsatisfactory performance procedure at the first stage (unless the failing constitutes gross incompetence). If more than one procedure is commenced, then, given that the procedures will relate to different failings and will have been identified at different times, the finding and outcome of each should be without prejudice to the others.

However, there may be circumstances where procedures have been initiated for a particular failing and an additional failing comes to light prior to the first stage meeting. In such circumstances it is possible to consolidate the two issues at the planned meeting provided that there is sufficient time prior to the meeting to comply with the notification requirements. Answer A is therefore incorrect.

If there is insufficient time to comply with the notification requirements (as was the case in this scenario), either the meeting should be rearranged to a date which allows the requirements to be met or a separate first stage meeting should be held in relation to the additional matter.

Therefore, Sergeant GREEGAN would have the option to adjourn the first stage meeting to discuss both matters at the same meeting, but should not discuss the additional matter at the planned meeting. Answer C is therefore incorrect.

On the other hand, there would be no requirement to wait until the officer reaches stage three of the unsatisfactory performance procedures to consolidate the unsatisfactory performance matters; this may be done at the first stage and answer D is therefore incorrect.

General Police Duties, para. 4.2.8

Answer 2.3

Answer **A** — The formal procedures to deal with unsatisfactory performance and attendance are set out in the Police (Performance) Regulations 2012. There are potentially three stages to the process, each of which involves a different meeting composition and possible outcomes. However, the process is the same whether the officer is being asked to account for their poor performance or their attendance. Answer C is therefore incorrect.

A line manager may ask a human resources professional or police officer (who should have experience of unsatisfactory performance procedures) to attend a meeting to advise him/her on the proceedings at the first stage meeting. Answer B is therefore incorrect. The line manager may also seek such advice before the meeting and answer C is also incorrect in this respect, because attendance at the meeting is optional and not mandatory.

If the experienced police officer is to attend the meeting, he/she must be independent of the line management chain (and not part of it at any level). Answer D is therefore incorrect.

General Police Duties, para. 4.2.9

Answer 2.4

Answer **D** — The purpose of the unsatisfactory performance procedures is to seek an improvement in performance and attendance; therefore, there is flexibility to achieve this aim.

A constable attending a first stage meeting is entitled to have a friend present. Answers A and C are therefore incorrect.

The line manager must provide the *police officer* or his/her *police friend* (if he/she has one) with an opportunity to make representations. The representations may be made verbally or in writing. Answers B and C are therefore incorrect for this reason also.

General Police Duties, para. 4.2.9.1

Answer 2.5

Answer **D** — It is expected that the specified period for improvement would not normally exceed three months. On the application of the police officer or otherwise (e.g. on the application of his/her line manager), the appropriate authority may extend the 'specified period' if it considers it appropriate to do so.

In setting an extension to the specified period, consideration should be given to any known periods of extended absence from the police officer's normal role, e.g. if the police officer is going to be on long periods of pre-planned holiday leave, study leave, or is due to undergo an operation. The extension should not lead to the improvement period exceeding 12 months; therefore, answers A and B are incorrect.

However, if the appropriate authority is satisfied that there are exceptional circumstances making it appropriate, the period may be extended beyond 12 months; therefore, answer C is incorrect.

General Police Duties, para. 4.2.9.2

Answer 2.6

Answer **C** — The 'validity period' of an improvement notice describes the period of 12 *months* from the date of the notice within which performance or attendance must be maintained (assuming improvement is made during the specified period). If the improvement is not maintained within this period, the next stage of the procedures may be used. Constable POUNDS has worked through a three-month action plan period and now has nine months of the 12 month 'validity period' left.

Answers A, B and D are therefore incorrect.

General Police Duties, para. 4.2.9.2

Answer 2.7

Answer **B** — There may be exceptional circumstances where the appropriate authority considers the performance of the police officer to be so unsatisfactory as to warrant the procedures being initiated at the third stage for 'gross incompetence'.

'Gross incompetence' is defined in the Police (Performance) Regulations 2012 as:

> ... a serious inability or serious failure of a police officer to perform the duties of the rank or role he is currently undertaking to a satisfactory standard or level, to the extent that dismissal would be justified, except that no account shall be taken of the attendance of a police officer when considering whether he has been grossly incompetent.

This Regulation is about performance and not attendance and answer C is therefore incorrect.

It is not envisaged that an appropriate authority would initiate the procedures at the third stage in respect of a series of acts over a period of time, whether similar or not; this Regulation is meant to deal with a *single* incident of 'gross incompetence'; therefore, answers A and D are incorrect.

General Police Duties, para. 4.2.11.1

Answer 2.8

Answer **C** — First, special constables may be required to attend a third stage meeting to deal with unsatisfactory performance. In arranging a third stage meeting involving special constables, due consideration should be given to the fact that special constables are unpaid volunteers and may therefore have full-time employment or other personal commitments. Answer A is therefore incorrect.

In cases where a special constable is required to attend a third stage meeting, the force will appoint a member of the special constabulary to attend the meeting to advise the panel (as opposed to the officer—this is for the purpose of fairness). Answer B is incorrect.

The special constable advising the panel must have sufficient seniority and experience of the special constabulary to be able to advise the panel; however, he/she will not form part of the panel and will not have a role in determining whether or not the police officer's performance or attendance is unsatisfactory. Answer D is therefore incorrect.

General Police Duties, para. 4.2.11.3

Answer 2.9

Answer **D** — Attendance at any stage meeting is not subject to the same considerations as reporting for duty and the provisions of reg. 33 (sick leave) of the Police Regulations 2003 do not apply. In other words, an officer may not claim that because he/she is unfit for duty, he/she is also unable to attend a meeting—of course, it will depend on the individual's illness, but a broken leg is a physical injury and should not prohibit the person from discussing a return to work plan. Answer B is therefore incorrect.

If the police officer is incapacitated, the meeting *may* be deferred until he/she is sufficiently improved to attend. Every effort should be made to make it *possible* for the police officer to attend; however, this is not mandatory and a meeting will not be deferred indefinitely because the police officer is unable to attend. Answer C is therefore incorrect.

Whilst the 2003 Regulations may not apply, advice and guidance suggest that the chair of the meeting should make efforts to help the officer to engage in the meeting, which could include holding the meeting at a location convenient to him/her. It will be the officer's force's duty to find a way to communicate with him/her and forcing the officer to attend a meeting will play into their hands, when it may be possible to communicate with them in some other way, such as using video, telephone or other conferencing technology. Answer A is therefore incorrect.

General Police Duties, para. 4.2.12

Answer 2.10

Answer **D** — There are several offences under the Police Act 1996 connected to such behaviour. First, there is impersonation under s. 90(1), but you would have to prove the person, with intent to deceive, impersonates a member of a police force or special constable, or makes any statement or does any act calculated falsely to suggest that he/she is such a member or constable. There is no clear evidence that this has happened in this question; therefore, answer A is incorrect.

There are further offences under the 1996 Act: under s. 90(2) (wearing an article of police uniform of a member of a police force as to be calculated to deceive) and s. 90(3) (possessing an article of police uniform).

Under subs. (3), a person can commit an offence by simply possessing the article of uniform unless he/she proves that he/she obtained possession of that article lawfully and has possession of it for a lawful purpose (which HEBDON cannot do in these circumstances). Answer C is incorrect because an offence may be committed even if the person has not tried to impersonate a police officer.

Finally, an 'article of police uniform' for the purposes of s. 90(3) includes any article of uniform, any distinctive badge or mark or any document of identification usually issued to members of police forces or special constables (s. 90(4)). HEBDON is guilty of this offence and answer B is incorrect.

General Police Duties, para. 4.2.17.2

3 | **Stop and Search**

QUESTIONS

Question 3.1

Constable DURAND was on patrol late at night and received a call concerning a person acting suspiciously near to a house. The control room informed the officer that neighbours had said that the premises had been unoccupied for about three months, following the death of the elderly occupant, and that the property was for sale. The officer attended immediately and found DRAKE in the rear garden of the house, hiding in some bushes. The officer decided to search DRAKE for stolen or prohibited articles.

> Did Constable DURAND have the power to search DRAKE under s. 1 of the Police and Criminal Evidence Act 1984, in these circumstances?

A No, searches in the garden of a dwelling are prohibited and the search was unlawful.

B Yes, DRAKE was in a garden of a house which was not being used as a dwelling and which was unoccupied; the search was lawful.

C No, searches must take place in a public place and the search was unlawful.

D Yes, there are no restrictions on searches which take place outside a dwelling; the search was lawful.

Question 3.2

Constable CORK attended a report of a theft in the High Street; a store detective had witnessed a female person removing two mobile phones from a display and walking out of the shop. The female was now being tracked by a CCTV operator, who reported that she was accompanied by two girls; one was about 5 years of age and the other was about 2 years of age, in a pushchair. As Constable CORK approached the suspect, she was told that she had placed one of the mobile phones in the older child's pocket and had hidden the other in the pushchair. Constable CORK detained the female and the two children.

Which of the following statements is correct, in relation to Constable CORK's power to search the two children, under s. 1 of the Police and Criminal Evidence Act 1984?

A Constable CORK could not search the children; because of their ages, they could not form the necessary criminal intent for this crime.

B Constable CORK could search the children, provided she had reasonable grounds to suspect she would find the stolen articles.

C Constable CORK could not search the children, because they are in innocent possession of stolen articles.

D Constable CORK could search the pushchair, because it is not a 'person'; however, she could not search the older child, because it could not form the necessary criminal intent for this crime.

Question 3.3

Constable LEE was on uniform mobile patrol and received a radio message from the control room. A member of the public had witnessed a theft from a vehicle and the suspect had got into a Renault car and driven off. A registration number was given and a short while later, Constable LEE was behind the vehicle. The officer stopped

3. Stop and Search

it and there was a single occupant, SAMPSON. The officer decided to search the Renault and SAMPSON.

In relation to the reasonable grounds for suspicion the officer would require before conducting a search, under s. 1 of the Police and Criminal Evidence Act 1984, which of the following statements is correct?

A Constable LEE could search the vehicle regardless of whether she suspected there was any likelihood of finding stolen articles.

B The information from the witness may provide reasonable grounds for suspicion; however, any grounds Constable LEE acted on should have been enough to give rise to reasonable suspicion in a 'reasonable person'.

C The information from the witness may provide reasonable grounds for suspicion; however, any grounds Constable LEE acted on should have been enough to give rise to reasonable suspicion in any person with similar skills to the officer.

D Constable LEE could search the vehicle regardless of whether she believed there was any likelihood of finding stolen articles, provided it could be shown that the *witness* had reasonable grounds to suspect there was a likelihood of finding stolen articles.

Question 3.4

An authorisation is in place under s. 60 of the Criminal Justice and Public Order Act 1994. There were serious riots and looting on the Friday night when the authorisation was granted. On the Saturday night, intelligence suggests that further riots will take place over the whole weekend and into the following week, with gang members carrying knives and other weapons. Superintendent LEACH is the senior officer in charge of policing for the area and is considering whether or not the s. 60 authorisation should be extended.

In relation to such an extension, which of the following statements is correct?

A Superintendent LEACH may extend the authorisation period, for up to seven days, depending on the intelligence.

B Superintendent LEACH may extend the authorisation period once, for a maximum period of 24 hours; further use of the powers would require a new authorisation.

C Superintendent LEACH may extend the authorisation period for 24 hours; further extensions may take place for 24-hour periods, up to a maximum of seven days.

D Superintendent LEACH may extend the authorisation period twice, for two 24-hour periods; further use of the powers would require a new authorisation.

Question 3.5

Constable WILLIS was on patrol in uniform in the early hours of the morning in an area where there had recently been outbreaks of serious public disorder between two gangs, who were known to carry weapons. An authorisation was in force, under s. 60 of the Criminal Justice and Public Order Act 1994, to stop and search persons in the locality. Constable WILLIS saw MOORE walking in the street wearing a ski mask, which was concealing his face.

In what circumstances could Constable WILLIS ask MOORE to remove his mask?

A If he reasonably believed that MOORE was likely to be involved in violence.

B No further circumstances are required, as an order is in force under s. 60.

C If he reasonably believed that MOORE was attempting to conceal his identity.

D If he reasonably believed that MOORE was carrying a dangerous instrument or an offensive weapon.

Question 3.6

A police control room received a report of a suspicious vehicle driving around at night. The informant stated that there were four male persons in the vehicle and that they were all wearing masks covering their faces. Constable BUNCE was on uniform mobile patrol and heard the observations for the vehicle. Shortly afterwards, the officer spotted the vehicle and began following it. Constable BUNCE was aware that there had recently been incidents of serious public disorder in the locality and that there was an order in force, under s. 60 of the Criminal Justice and Public Order Act 1994, to stop and search persons for weapons. It was dark and Constable BUNCE could not tell whether the occupants were wearing masks or not, but the officer intended stopping the vehicle to establish if they were.

What powers would be available to Constable BUNCE under s. 60AA of the Criminal Justice and Public Order Act 1994 (requirement to remove items worn for the purpose of concealing identity), in these circumstances?

A Constable BUNCE has the power to stop the vehicle under s. 60AA, in order to require the occupants to remove their masks.

B Constable BUNCE would have to use the general power under s. 163 of the Road Traffic Act 1988 to stop the vehicle; however, there is a power to search a vehicle for items used to conceal a person's identity under s. 60AA.

C Constable BUNCE has the power to stop the vehicle under s. 60AA, in order to require the occupants to remove their masks, or to search the vehicle for such items, if they are not wearing any.

D Constable BUNCE would have to use the general power under s. 163 of the Road Traffic Act 1988 to stop the vehicle; there is no power to search a vehicle for items used to conceal a person's identity under s. 60AA.

Question 3.7

DCs SHELBY and MINTO have attended at KHAN's home address to serve a Terrorism Prevention and Investigation Measures (TPIM) notice on him under s. 2 of the Terrorism Prevention and Investigation Measures Act 2011, to restrict his movements because of his suspected links to terrorism. The officers are considering searching KHAN when the notice has been served to ascertain whether there is anything on him that contravenes the measures specified in the notice.

Which of the following statements is correct, in relation to any reasonable suspicion the officers must have, before such a search can take place?

A If they are in possession of a warrant accompanying the notice, they do not require any reasonable grounds to suspect that KHAN has anything on him that contravenes the measures specified in the notice.

B They do not require any reasonable grounds to suspect that KHAN has anything on him that contravenes the measures specified in the notice, regardless of whether or not they have a warrant.

C They require reasonable grounds to suspect that KHAN is in possession of articles connected with terrorism.

D They require reasonable grounds to suspect that KHAN is in possession of articles that could be used to threaten or harm any person.

Question 3.8

MIAH has previously been served with a Terrorism Prevention and Investigation Measures (TPIM) notice, under s. 2 of the Terrorism Prevention and Investigation Measures Act 2011. The police are in possession of intelligence that MIAH has obtained a mobile phone and has been communicating with people abroad, over the Internet. This is contrary to the measures specified in the TPIM notice. The intelligence suggests he is using the phone whilst away from his home and the police have obtained a warrant to search MIAH for the phone.

Which of the following statements is correct, in relation to the measures that must be taken in order to conduct the search?

A The police may search MIAH on one occasion, within 28 days of the warrant being issued.

B There is no time limit in which the police have to perform the search, but they may only conduct it once.

C The police may search MIAH on more than one occasion if it is necessary to do so, but must do so within 28 days of the warrant being issued.

D The police may search MIAH on one occasion, within three months of the warrant being issued.

Question 3.9

DUNN was stopped in the street by Constables MEEK and PHELAN, both male officers. The officers had reasonable suspicion that DUNN was in possession of stolen jewellery, as they had been conducting surveillance on him. They believed that the jewellery was contained in a clear bag, hidden in his trousers, or possibly his underwear. While they were speaking to him, a police van pulled up to see if they needed assistance. The officers wish to search DUNN by requiring him to remove his trousers or if necessary his underwear and thereby expose intimate body parts.

To what extent could the officers search DUNN in these circumstances?

A They could require DUNN to remove items of clothing that would involve the exposure of intimate body parts in the rear of the police van, provided it is out of public view.

B They would have to take DUNN to a nearby police station if they want to remove his underwear and expose intimate body parts.

C They could take DUNN to a nearby police station, or another nearby location which is out of public view, if they want to remove his underwear and expose intimate body parts.

D They could not remove DUNN's underwear anywhere; this would be a strip search which may not carried out under s. 1 of PACE.

Question 3.10

Constable DANIELLS, a male officer, and Constable NEVIN, a female officer, stopped BENTLEY in the car park of a shopping centre. The officers had reasonable suspicion that BENTLEY was in possession of stolen goods, having received information from a CCTV operator who had seen her shoplifting. The officers were in a police van at the time and had been told that BENTLEY was possibly hiding a stolen necklace in her coat pocket.

Which of the following statements is correct, according to the PACE Codes of Practice, in relation to searching BENTLEY?

A Only Constable NEVIN could search BENTLEY in these circumstances.
B Either officer could search BENTLEY, provided they were only searching her outer garments.
C Either officer could search BENTLEY, provided they were only searching her outer garments and the search took place out of public view.
D Only Constable NEVIN could search BENTLEY in these circumstances, although the search could take place in the presence of Constable DANIELLS.

Question 3.11

Constable BAIRD attended a suspicious incident reported by POOLE, a CCTV operator. POOLE saw two men acting suspiciously near a 4 × 4 vehicle, and saw one of the men hand the other a bag of white powder. He believed the bag was placed inside the cover of the spare wheel attached to the rear door of the vehicle. As a result of this information, Constable BAIRD attended the scene. When the officer arrived, the two men were not with the vehicle—it was unattended. Constable BAIRD searched the spare wheel, but found nothing inside.

Is Constable BAIRD required to supply a notice of this search, under s. 2 of the Police and Criminal Evidence Act 1984?

A Yes, it should be placed on the vehicle, and a copy sent to the registered owner.
B No, a notice is not required as the inside of the vehicle was not searched.
C Yes, it should be placed inside the vehicle, which may be entered by force to do so.
D Yes, a notice must be placed somewhere on the vehicle.

Question 3.12

Inspector SPINK receives high-quality intelligence from a trusted source that there is going to be a large fight between two gangs of men (armed with knives, baseball bats and other offensive weapons) outside the Saddlers Arms pub. The source states that one of the gangs (numbering approximately 20 men) will be arriving in a coach and provides the registration number of the coach. Inspector SPINK reasonably believes it is necessary to authorise the use of the power under s. 60 of the Criminal Justice Act 1994 to stop and search the coach and its occupants as it approaches the pub in order to prevent serious violence taking place.

Would Inspector SPINK be able to authorise the use of the power under s. 60 in these circumstances?

A Yes, although any authorisation given would be subject to an initial authorisation limit of 15 hours.

B No, the power can only be authorised by an officer of the rank of superintendent or above.

C Yes, although any authorisation given would be subject to an initial authorisation limit of 24 hours.

D No, the power can only be authorised by an officer of the rank of assistant chief constable (or commander in the Metropolitan Police or City of London Police).

Question 3.13

A trade dispute has broken out over the sacking of several members of staff working for Portan Holdings Ltd. The company owns two large factory premises located approximately 1 mile away from each other in separate police force areas. Protesters have gathered at both factory premises to demonstrate their opposition to the sackings and reliable information is received that some of the protesters are intent on causing trouble, planning to attack any member of the Portan Holdings Ltd management team they see and cause them serious injury. To achieve that aim, they have taken a number of offensive weapons to both factory premises and are waiting outside the premises. Consideration is being given to authorising the powers under s. 60 of the Criminal Justice and Public Order Act 1994 to cover the factories concerned and the areas surrounding them.

Could the power be authorised in this situation?

A No, as no incidents of serious violence have actually taken place.

B Yes, an officer from either of the police forces where the factories are located can authorise the power in both police force areas, as the grounds for such an authorisation are connected.

C No, as an authorisation under s. 60 of the Act must cover an entire force area rather than a smaller part of it.

D Yes, but as the power is to be used in response to a threat or incident that straddles police force areas, an officer from each of the forces concerned will need to give an authorisation.

Question 3.14

DC FISHLOCK (dressed in plain clothes) has attended the scene of a large public disorder incident. During the course of the disorder, an offence of wounding (contrary to s. 18 of the Offences Against the Person Act 1861) took place. The wounding offence occurred in the last 30 minutes and involved the victim being stabbed several times with a knife. In order to recover the weapon concerned, an authorisation under s. 60 of the Criminal Justice and Police Act 1994 has been granted. Whilst DC FISHLOCK is making enquiries in the street where the wounding took place, he sees OSBORN walking towards him; OSBORN is wearing a black mask which partially covers his face. DC FISHLOCK believes OSBORN is wearing the mask wholly for the purpose of concealing his identity.

Would DC FISHLOCK be able to use the power under s. 60AA of the Criminal Justice and Public Order 1994 and require OSBORN to remove the mask and seize it?

A Yes, because DC FISHLOCK believes OSBORN is wearing the mask wholly for the purpose of concealing his identity.

B No, because the power under s. 60AA is only exercisable by an officer in uniform.

C Yes, because the powers under s. 60 of the Act have been authorised, this automatically means that the powers under s. 60AA of the Act are also available.

D No, because the only way the powers under s. 60AA of the Act would be available would be if they had been specifically authorised, i.e. subject to a 'stand-alone' authorisation.

Question 3.15

BARR is driving a Volkswagen Passat motor vehicle (owned by LOMBARDI). BARR parks the vehicle on the car park of the Hound pub, enters the pub and strikes up a conversation with STRANG (who, unknown to BARR, is a well-known handler of stolen goods). After having a drink, BARR leaves the pub, gets back into the Passat and drives off. Once he is out of sight of the pub, he is stopped by PC GUMBLE (who is on uniform mobile patrol) as the police have been keeping observations on STRANG inside the pub and suspect that he has sold stolen property to BARR. PC GUMBLE searches BARR and the Passat for stolen property (under s. 1 of the Police and Criminal Evidence Act 1984); no stolen property is found. PC GUMBLE fills out a single search record in respect of the search and provides a copy of it to BARR.

Has PC GUMBLE correctly followed the provisions of Code A of the Codes of Practice?

A No, as a separate search record is required for the search of BARR and the search of the vehicle.

B Yes, as the object and grounds for the search are the same, only one search record needs to be completed.

C No, as BARR is not the owner of the vehicle, a copy of the search record of the vehicle must also be sent to LOMBARDI (the owner of the vehicle) within three months from the date of the search.

D Yes, although LOMBARDI (as the owner of the vehicle searched) is entitled to a copy of the search record if she applies for it within three months from the date of the search.

Question 3.16

PC PORTER is on uniform foot patrol when he is directed to an area where a burglary has just taken place. A description of the possible offender is circulated and while searching the area, PC PORTER sees MALIK, who matches the description circulated, walking towards him. PC PORTER decides to exercise his powers under s. 1 of the Police and Criminal Evidence Act 1984 and to search MALIK. When PC PORTER approaches and speaks to MALIK, it becomes obvious that MALIK is having difficulty understanding what the officer is saying to him.

With regard to the Police and Criminal Evidence Act 1984, which of the following statements is correct?

A As MALIK does not appear to understand what is being said to him, PC PORTER cannot search him.

B PC PORTER must give MALIK certain information which can be communicated before or during the course of the search.

C As MALIK does not appear to understand what is being said, PC PORTER must take reasonable steps to bring all relevant information to his attention before starting the search.

D As MALIK is having difficulty understanding what PC PORTER is saying, the officer need not attempt to explain anything to him and he may search MALIK without communicating the usual information required.

Question 3.17

PC ASHCROFT (a male officer) and PC HOLLAND (a female officer) are on uniform mobile patrol in a marked police van which has no windows in the rear so the inside of the van cannot be seen from the street. They are directed to attend an incident of burglary where the offender has stolen a large amount of property including a mobile phone, watch and wallet. A description of the suspect is circulated and as the officers get closer to the scene of the offence they see TYLER (a male), who closely matches the description of the suspect, running along a street. The officers manage to stop TYLER and are considering whether to search him using the power under s. 1 of the Police and Criminal Evidence Act 1984 as they reasonably suspect they will find stolen articles on TYLER's person.

Thinking about the issues in respect of s. 1 of the Police and Criminal Evidence Act 1984 and Code A of the Codes of Practice, which of the following comments is correct?

A If the search involves the removal of no more than TYLER's outer coat, jacket and gloves then either officer could carry out a search of TYLER in the street in those circumstances.

B As TYLER is a male, only PC ASHCROFT could carry out a s. 1 search in these circumstances.

C The officers could place TYLER in the rear of the police vehicle and require him to remove his T-shirt but only if both officers are present.

D If it were necessary, a search involving the exposure of TYLER's intimate parts could take place in the rear of the police vehicle (as long as PC HOLLAND is not present).

ANSWERS

Answer 3.1

Answer **B** — Under s. 1(2) of the Police and Criminal Evidence Act 1984, a constable:

(a) may search—
  (i) any person or vehicle;
  (ii) anything which is in or on a vehicle, for stolen or prohibited articles or any article to which subsection (8A) below applies or any firework to which subsection (8B) below applies; and
(b) may detain a person or vehicle for the purpose of such a search.

Searches in gardens of dwellings are not prohibited altogether; under s. 1(4), where a person is in a garden or yard occupied with and used for the purposes of a dwelling or on other land so occupied and used, a constable may not search him/her in the exercise of the power conferred by this section unless the constable has reasonable grounds for believing:

(a) that he/she does not reside in the dwelling; and
(b) that he/she is not in the place in question with the express or implied permission of a person who resides in the dwelling.

Answers A and C are therefore incorrect.

There *are* restrictions on searches which take place outside a dwelling by virtue of s. 1(4); therefore, answer D is incorrect.

General Police Duties, paras 4.3.4.1, 4.3.4.2

Answer 3.2

Answer **B** — Under s. 1(2) of the Police and Criminal Evidence Act 1984, a constable:

(a) may search—
  (i) any person or vehicle;
  (ii) anything which is in or on a vehicle, for stolen or prohibited articles or any article to which subsection (8A) below applies or any firework to which subsection (8B) below applies; and
(b) may detain a person or vehicle for the purpose of such a search.

Paragraph 2.2A of Code A states that:

> The exercise of these stop and search powers depends on the likelihood that the person searched is in possession of an item for which they may be searched; it does not depend on the person concerned being suspected of committing an offence in relation to the object of the search.

Paragraph 2.2A further states that a police officer who has reasonable grounds to suspect that a person is in innocent possession of a stolen or prohibited article, controlled drug or other item for which the officer is empowered to search, may stop and search the person even though there would be no power of arrest. Answers C and D are therefore incorrect.

This would even apply when a child under the age of criminal responsibility (10 years) is suspected of carrying any such item, even if they knew they had it. Answers A and D are incorrect for this reason also.

General Police Duties, paras 4.3.4.1, 4.3.4.3

Answer 3.3

Answer **B** — Under Code C of the PACE Codes of practice, para. 2.1(a), a constable must have reasonable grounds to suspect that the relevant articles would be found, before the powers under s. 1 of the Police and Criminal Evidence Act 1984 can be exercised.

The courts have accepted that reasonable grounds for suspicion can arise from information given to the officer by a colleague, an informant or even anonymously (*O'Hara* v *Chief Constable of the Royal Ulster Constabulary* [1997] AC 286). There is no requirement to prove that the witness had a reasonable suspicion, or whether they had any particular skills and answers C and D are incorrect.

The courts have held that it must be shown that any such grounds on which an officer acted would have been enough to give rise to that suspicion in a 'reasonable person' (*Nakkuda Ali* v *Jayaratne* [1951] AC 66).

However, the mere existence of such circumstances or evidence is not enough. The officer must actually have a 'reasonable suspicion' that the relevant articles will be found. If, in fact, the officer knows that there is little or no likelihood of finding the articles, the power could not be used (*R* v *Harrison* [1938] 3 All ER 134). Answer A is therefore incorrect.

General Police Duties, paras 4.3.4.3, 4.3.4.4

Answer 3.4

Answer **B** — Under s. 60 of the Criminal Justice and Public Order Act 1994, if an inspector reasonably believes that incidents of serious violence may take place in his/her area, or that people are carrying dangerous instruments or offensive weapons, he/she may give an authorisation to stop any pedestrian and search him/her for offensive weapons or dangerous instruments.

A direction to *extend* the period authorised under the power may be given only once. This extension is for a maximum period of 24 hours and thereafter further use of the powers requires a new authorisation. In the context of this question, the extension may be granted on the Saturday night, but if intelligence suggests further incidents will take place on the Sunday and Monday night, a new authorisation may be put in place on the Sunday, which can be extended to the Monday if necessary.

Answers A, C and D are incorrect for these reasons.

General Police Duties, paras 4.3.4.5, 4.3.4.6

Answer 3.5

Answer **C** — Under s. 60AA(1) of the Criminal Justice and Public Order Act 1994, where an authorisation under s. 60 is in force, a constable in uniform may require any person to remove any item which the constable reasonably believes that person is wearing wholly or mainly for the purpose of concealing his/her identity. The power is not absolute, as the constable has reasonably to believe that the person is wearing the item to conceal his/her identity (therefore, answer B is incorrect). There is no need, however, for the constable reasonably to believe that the person is carrying a dangerous instrument or an offensive weapon, or that the person is likely to be involved in violence, in order to exercise the power under s. 60AA(1). Those matters would have been considered before the authorisation was granted under s. 60. Answers A and D are therefore incorrect.

General Police Duties, para. 4.3.4.9

Answer 3.6

Answer **D** — Under s. 60AA of the Criminal Justice and Public Order Act 1994, where an authorisation under s. 60 is in force, a constable in uniform may require any person to remove any item which the constable reasonably believes that person is wearing wholly or mainly for the purpose of concealing his/her identity. However, unlike

s. 60, there is no specific power under this section to stop vehicles and therefore answers A and C are incorrect.

There is also no power to search for face coverings etc. under s. 60AA. The Divisional Court has held that the predecessor to this power (the old s. 60(4A)) neither involved nor required a 'search' and that, therefore, the provisions of s. 2 of the Police and Criminal Evidence Act 1984 did not apply (*DPP* v *Avery* [2001] EWHC 748 (Admin)). The court went on to hold that, although the power amounted to a significant interference with a person's liberty, it was justified by the type of situation envisaged by the legislators, whereby the police may need to call upon the law. Clearly, if an item is found during a lawful search for other articles (say, under s. 60(4)) which does not require any 'reasonable belief' by the officer, face coverings and masks could then be seized under s. 60AA(2)(b). As there is no accompanying power of search under s. 60AA, answer B is incorrect.

Given that this is a power for police officers in uniform, the general power to stop vehicles under s. 163 of the Road Traffic Act 1988 could be used.

General Police Duties, paras 4.3.4.9, 4.3.4.13

Answer 3.7

Answer **B** — Paragraph 3 of sch. 5 to the Terrorism Prevention and Investigation Measures Act 2011 allows a constable to detain an individual to be searched under the following powers:

- para. 6(2)(a) when a TPIM notice is being, or has just been, served on the individual for the purpose of ascertaining whether there is anything on the individual that contravenes measures specified in the notice;
- para. 8(2)(a) in accordance with a warrant to search the individual if that search is necessary to determine whether an individual is complying with measures specified in the notice (see para. 2.20); and
- para. 10 to ascertain whether an individual in respect of whom a TPIM notice is in force is in possession of anything that could be used to threaten or harm any person.

The officers in the question are exercising their powers under para. 6(2)(a)—serving a TPIM notice without a warrant—which allows them to search KHAN.

Paragraph 2.19 of the PACE Code of Practice in relation to sch. 5 states that when exercising his/her powers of search, there is no requirement for the constable to have reasonable grounds to suspect that the individual has been, or is, contravening any of the measures specified in the TPIM notice; or is not complying with measures specified in the TPIM notice; or is in possession of anything that could be used to threaten or harm any person.

In summary, the officers can simply search KAHN because they are attending to serve the TPIM notice on him, and answers A, C and D are incorrect.

General Police Duties, para. 4.3.4.14

Answer 3.8

Answer **A** — Paragraph 8(2)(a) of sch. 5 to the Terrorism Prevention and Investigation Measures Act 2011 allows a constable to detain and search an individual in accordance with a warrant, if that search is necessary to determine whether an individual is complying with measures specified in the notice.

Paragraph 2.20 of the PACE Code of Practice in relation to sch. 5 states that a search of an individual on warrant under the power mentioned must be carried out within 28 days of the issue of the warrant and:

- the individual may be searched on one occasion only within that period;
- the search must take place at a reasonable hour unless it appears that this would frustrate the purposes of the search.

This means that answer A is correct, and answers B, C and D are incorrect.

General Police Duties, para. 4.3.4.14

Answer 3.9

Answer **C** — Code C, para. 3.5 of the PACE Codes of Practice states that there is no power to *require* a person to remove any clothing *in public* other than an outer coat, jacket or gloves (except under s. 60AA of the Criminal Justice and Public Order Act 1994, which empowers a constable to require a person to remove any item worn to conceal identity).

Paragraph 3.6 states that where, on reasonable grounds, it is considered necessary to conduct a more thorough search (e.g. by requiring a person to take off a T-shirt or trousers), this must be done out of public view, for example in a police van or police station if there is one nearby.

Paragraph 3.7 states that searches involving exposure of intimate parts of the body may be carried out only at a nearby police station *or other nearby location* which is out of public view (but not a police vehicle). Answers A and B are therefore incorrect.

This paragraph goes on to say that a search involving exposure of intimate parts of the body must be conducted in accordance with the requirements of Annex A to Code C (strip searches), but that an intimate search may not be authorised or carried out under any stop and search powers. However, what the officers propose to do amounts to a strip search only (intimate searches involve searching body orifices other than the mouth) and this *may* be conducted under s. 1, at either of the locations described previously. Answer D is therefore incorrect.

General Police Duties, para. 4.3.5

Answer 3.10

Answer **B** — Code C, para. 3.5 of the PACE Codes of Practice states that there is no power to require a person to remove any clothing in public other than an outer coat, jacket or gloves (except under s. 60AA of the Criminal Justice and Public Order Act 1994, which empowers a constable to require a person to remove any item worn to conceal identity).

A search in public of a person's clothing which has not been removed must be restricted to superficial examination of outer garments. This does not, however, prevent an officer from placing his/her hand inside the pockets of the outer clothing, or feeling round the inside of collars, socks and shoes if this is reasonably necessary in the circumstances to look for the object of the search or to remove and examine any item reasonably suspected to be the object of the search. For the same reasons, subject to the restrictions on the removal of headgear, a person's hair may also be searched in public.

The only time the gender of the officer is mentioned in this Code is when it relates to conducting a more thorough search. Paragraph 3.6 states that where on reasonable grounds it is considered necessary to conduct a more thorough search (e.g. by requiring a person to take off a T-shirt), this must be done out of public view, for example in a police van or police station if there is one nearby.

This paragraph goes on to say that any search involving the removal of more than an outer coat, jacket, gloves, headgear or footwear, or any other item concealing identity, may only be made by an officer of the same sex as the person searched and may not be made in the presence of anyone of the opposite sex unless the person being searched specifically requests it.

This means that Constable DANIELLS *could* go through BENTLEY's pockets, according to Code C, but if the item is not found and a more thorough search is required, the male officer may not be present or conduct the search. Answers A and D are therefore incorrect.

There is no requirement to conduct a search of outer garments out of public view and answer C is incorrect.

Note that this question is simply a matter of what is written in Code C; it may be that some forces have a policy which prohibits officers searching people of the opposite sex and care would need to be taken not to breach the Equality Act 2010. However, in the circumstances, there would be nothing wrong with asking BENTLEY to take her coat off so that the pockets may be searched by either officer.

General Police Duties, para. 4.3.5

Answer 3.11

Answer **D** — Section 2(6) of the Police and Criminal Evidence Act 1984 states that 'on completing the search of an unattended vehicle, or anything in or on such a vehicle, a constable shall leave a notice'. Therefore, even though the spare tyre was not actually in the vehicle, a notice must be left, and for that reason answer B is incorrect.

There may be occasions when officers have to force entry into a vehicle in order to search it. On such an occasion, the officer must, if practicable, leave the vehicle secure (Code A, para. 4.10). However, where the vehicle has not been damaged during the search, s. 2(7) states that 'the constable shall leave the notice inside the vehicle unless it is not reasonably practicable to do so without damaging the vehicle'. Answer C is therefore incorrect.

There is no obligation on the officer to send a notice to the registered owner's address, and therefore answer A is incorrect.

General Police Duties, para. 4.3.5.2

Answer 3.12

Answer **C** — The power under s. 60 of the Criminal Justice and Public Order Act 1994 can be authorised by an officer of the rank of inspector or above, making answers B and D incorrect. The initial authorisation of the power can last up to 24 hours (correct answer C), making answer A incorrect.

General Police Duties, paras 4.3.4.4, 4.3.4.5

Answer 3.13

Answer **D** — An authorisation under s. 60 can be given if a police officer of or above the rank of inspector reasonably believes that:

- incidents involving serious violence may take place in any locality in his/her police area, and that it is expedient to give an authorisation under this section to prevent their occurrence; or
- an incident involving serious violence has taken place in England and Wales in his/her police area and that a dangerous instrument or offensive weapon used in the incident is being carried in any locality in his/her police area by a person and it is expedient to give an authorisation under this section to find the instrument or weapon; or
- persons are carrying dangerous instruments or offensive weapons in any locality in his/her police area without good reason, he/she may give an authorisation that the powers conferred by this section are to be exercisable at any place within that locality for a specified period not exceeding 24 hours.

The authorisation is not limited to situations where incidents of serious violence have taken place, making answer A incorrect.

It is for the authorising officer to determine the geographical area in which the use of the powers is to be authorised (this may encompass an entire police force area, but not necessarily so), making answer C incorrect. If the area specified is smaller than the whole force area, the officer giving the authorisation should specify either the streets which form the boundary of the area or a divisional boundary within the force area.

Answer B is incorrect as if the power is to be used in response to a threat or incident that straddles police force areas, an officer from *each* of the forces concerned will need to give an authorisation (correct answer D).

General Police Duties, para. 4.3.4.6

Answer 3.14

Answer **B** — The powers under s. 60AA can be authorised as a 'stand-alone' power, but they are also available when the powers under s. 60 of the Criminal Justice and Public Order Act 1994 are authorised. This means that when a s. 60 authorisation is made, the powers under s. 60AA of the Act are also automatically available, meaning that answer D is incorrect. This would seem to make answer C correct—that is not the case. It is correct that the powers under s. 60AA would be available in the area where the s. 60 has been granted, but the important element here is that the powers under s. 60 (and s. 60AA) are only granted to an officer in uniform. So the fact that the powers under s. 60AA are available and the fact that DC FISHLOCK believes OSBORN is wearing the mask wholly for the purpose of concealing his identity are irrelevant (answers A and C are incorrect). If DC FISHLOCK were in uniform then the officer could use the power—*he is not* so the power is not available to the officer.

General Police Duties, paras 4.3.4.8 to 4.3.4.11

Answer 3.15

Answer **B** — A record is required for each person and each vehicle searched. However, answer A is incorrect as if a person is in a vehicle and both are searched, and the object and the grounds for the search are the same, only one record need be completed (correct answer B (Code A, para. 4.5)). So in these circumstances PC GUMBLE would comply with Code A of the Codes of Practice. The owner of the vehicle searched is not mentioned by Code A of the Code of Practice (only the person in charge of the vehicle)—the owner of the vehicle is not provided with any entitlement to a copy of the record of search so answers C and D are incorrect.

General Police Duties, para. 4.3.6.1

Answer 3.16

Answer **C** — Code A of the Codes of Practice (para. 3.11) states that if a person does not appear to understand what is being said, or there is any doubt about their ability to understand English, the officer must take all reasonable steps to bring the relevant information (constable's name, etc.) to the person's attention, making answer D incorrect. The relevant information must be given *before* starting the search (making answer B incorrect). The fact that MALIK does not understand the officer does not preclude the use of the powers under s. 1 of the Police and Criminal Evidence Act 1984, making answer A incorrect.

General Police Duties, para. 4.3.5.1

Answer 3.17

Answer **A** — There would be nothing wrong with an everyday s. 1 search taking place in the street in such circumstances. The officers reasonably suspect that they will find stolen articles on TYLER and have legitimate justification for the use of the power. When the power is being used to carry out a search that involves the removal of no more than the outer coat, jacket and gloves etc. then a male may search a female and vice versa (answer A). There is no requirement for such a search to made by a person of the same sex, making answer B incorrect. Answer C is incorrect as if the officers did

3. Stop and Search

require TYLER to remove his T-shirt this would have to be done out of the public domain and only by an officer of the same sex. Officers or persons of the opposite sex may not be present unless the person searched specifically requests it. Answer D is incorrect as a search involving intimate body parts cannot take place in a police vehicle.

General Police Duties, para. 4.3.5

4 | Entry, Search and Seizure

STUDY PREPARATION

In the previous chapter, we examined the powers to search people and vehicles for evidence of an offence. This chapter deals with the powers to enter and search *premises* either to seize evidence of an offence, or to arrest a person. These powers generally fall into two categories:

1. search of premises under the authority of a warrant;
2. search of premises without the authority of a warrant.

Knowing and understanding these powers leads to confidence, not just as a student or exam candidate but as a police officer generally.

QUESTIONS

Question 4.1

Police officers entered premises under the authority of a warrant issued under the Misuse of Drugs Act 1971. The premises were empty when the warrant was executed and while they were conducting the search for evidence relating to the unlawful supply of controlled substances, they came across other property which appeared to be stolen. A discussion took place as to how the officers should deal with the property, as it was not covered in the warrant and the original reason for the search.

Which of the following statements is correct in relation to the correct application of the officers' powers, and how they should deal with the suspected stolen property?

A The purpose of the entry was to find evidence relating to the unlawful supply of controlled drugs; officers may not seize suspected stolen goods in these circumstances.

B The purpose of the entry was to find evidence relating to the unlawful supply of controlled drugs; officers would require an additional authorisation under the Police and Criminal Evidence Act 1984, to seize suspected stolen goods in these circumstances.

C Provided the original entry by the officers was lawful, they may seize suspected stolen goods while on the premises, even if that was not the original purpose for entry.

D Provided the original entry by the officers was lawful, they may only seize other goods while on the premises which are connected with, or similar to, the offence suspected, even if that was not the original purpose for entry.

Question 4.2

DCs COHEN and VARDY work on a specialist team investigating organised crime groups in their region. PEARSON was arrested for a series of armed robberies and was in police detention; a search of his office premises was authorised under s. 18 of the Police and Criminal Evidence Act 1984 (PACE). The officers attended the office premises owned by PEARSON to search for evidence connecting him to the robberies. At the premises, they produced a copy of the search authorisation to MANNINGS, who worked for PEARSON. MANNINGS pointed out to the officers that their names did not appear on the authorisation and demanded they disclose who they were and the station they worked at before they conducted the search.

Which of the following statements is correct, in relation to the searches of premises, under Code B of the PACE Codes of Practice?

A MANNINGS is entitled to know the officers' identities before the search; they should either be disclosed on the PACE authorisation or the officers should identify themselves.

B The officers' identities should be disclosed unless they reasonably believe that recording or disclosing their names might put them in danger.

C The officers are not investigating a case linked to terrorism, where it is reasonably believed that recording or disclosing their names might put them in danger; therefore, their identities must be disclosed.

D The officers' identities should be disclosed unless an inspector has authorised in writing that he/she reasonably believes that recording or disclosing their names might put them in danger.

Question 4.3

DC HALL is investigating an allegation that FRISK, who owns a building company, paid bribes to officers in a local authority planning department over a number of years, to push through planning applications. DC HALL has recovered evidence from a search of FRISK's offices and anticipates seizing numerous documents and computers at the local authority offices. DC HALL is seeking a multiple entry search warrant, but is uncertain how many visits will be required to complete the evidence-gathering process.

Which of the following statements is correct, in relation to the type of warrant DC HALL is seeking?

A DC HALL must state the maximum number of entries desired in the application for the warrant.

B DC HALL may apply for a warrant authorising unlimited entries in these circumstances, because the maximum number is unknown.

C DC HALL is not required to specify the number of entries desired; the warrant will automatically authorise unlimited entries.

D DC HALL is not required to specify the number of entries desired; an inspector may authorise further entries if necessary.

Question 4.4

DC GRANT is investigating a case involving a series of frauds. The officer has obtained an all premises warrant which authorises the search of PEDERSON's office and home address. DC GRANT has recovered documents that suggest PEDERSON owns two other premises where evidence may be found.

Will the warrant in DC GRANT's possession authorise the search of the other two premises?

A Yes, provided entry to those premises is authorised by an inspector in writing.

B Yes, provided entry to those premises is authorised by a superintendent in writing.

C No, DC GRANT will have to apply to a magistrate for another all premises warrant to search those premises.

D Yes, provided entry to those premises is authorised by an inspector in writing, or if one is not readily available, the senior officer on duty.

Question 4.5

DC GOMEZ was the officer in charge of a search which was conducted at MALONEY's home address. Officers entered the premises by force under the authority of a warrant to search for property stolen from a recent burglary at a jeweller's shop. The search team found several items of jewellery matching the description of the stolen goods and these were seized as evidence. MALONEY was not present when the search took place and DC GOMEZ established that there was no other person available who appeared to be in charge of the premises; however, the officer forgot to leave a copy of the warrant in a prominent place in the premises.

Given that DC GOMEZ has failed to follow the requirements of s. 16(7) of PACE by not leaving a copy of the warrant in a prominent place, which of the following statements is correct?

A The search was unlawful; this may result in the exclusion of any evidence obtained under the warrant and officers could be made to return the jewellery to MALONEY.

B This is a minor deviation from the terms of the warrant which would not render the search unlawful or result in the exclusion of any evidence obtained.

C The search was unlawful; this may result in the exclusion of any evidence obtained under the warrant, but officers could not be made to return the jewellery to MALONEY.

D The search was unlawful, but a failure to follow the requirements of s. 16 will not result in the exclusion of any evidence obtained under the warrant.

Question 4.6

A number of large parties have been taking place on weekends and officers suspect that COOKSLEY is the organiser. The location of the events changes every week and intelligence suggests that COOKSLEY is dealing Class A drugs from a tent that is erected at each venue, which also contains the sound equipment for the parties. Officers have information that COOKSLEY transports the equipment and drugs to the venues in the back of a van. They are considering applying for a warrant under the Misuse of Drugs Act 1971 to search the vehicle and tent for drugs. However, COOKSLEY's address is unknown and officers will have to wait until the following weekend for intelligence on the next venue.

Which of the following statements is correct, in relation to the officers' intentions?

A Only the tent is a 'premises' in respect of a search warrant; there is no power to apply for a warrant to search a vehicle in this way.

B Both the tent and the vehicle are 'premises' and officers could apply for a search warrant in respect of both.

C Neither the tent (which is a moveable structure) nor the vehicle are 'premises' in respect of a search warrant; officers will have to use other powers to search them.

D Officers will have to use other powers to search both the tent and the vehicle; a search warrant requires a location to be specified in it before one can be issued.

Question 4.7

DC PRICE is investigating a fraud case and has uncovered evidence that a number of solicitors from a local firm may be involved. The officer has applied to a justice of the peace for a warrant under s. 8 of the Police and Criminal Evidence Act 1984, to enter and search the solicitors' offices for evidence relating to the offence. DC PRICE has reasonable cause to believe that there may be communications between solicitors and clients referring to the fraud. The officer is aware that there may be a substantial amount of paper and computer records on the premises and is anticipating having to use powers under s. 50 of the Criminal Justice and Police Act 2001 to seize and sift evidence.

Which of the following statements is correct, in relation to items subject to legal privilege which may be on the premises?

A Any communication between solicitors and clients is subject to legal privilege and cannot be searched for or seized under the terms of a warrant.

B Any items found that relate to criminal offences are not subject to legal privilege and may be searched for or seized.

C A warrant cannot authorise a search for legally privileged material and if such material is inadvertently seized, it would render the search unlawful.

D The possession of a warrant under s. 8 authorises any material found on the premises to be seized and sifted.

Question 4.8

Late at night, Constable CLYNE was in uniform following a motor vehicle on a road, which was not displaying any lights. The officer activated the sirens and blue lights to the police vehicle, attempting to get the other vehicle to stop. However, the other vehicle accelerated away from Constable CLYNE and was lost after a period of time.

4. Entry, Search and Seizure

About an hour later, the officer attended the address of the registered owner of the vehicle. The vehicle concerned was found outside the address and Constable CLYNE knocked on the door to speak to the occupant(s)—there was no reply. There were lights on at the premises and Constable CLYNE believed that the driver was inside the premises.

> Given that Constable CLYNE may have had reasonable grounds for believing that the driver was on the premises, was there a power of entry in these circumstances?

A No, the driver had not been involved in an accident which involved injury to any person.

B Yes, the driver of the vehicle failed to stop when required to do so by a constable in uniform.

C No, Constable CLYNE was not in immediate pursuit of the driver of the vehicle.

D Yes, but only if Constable CLYNE had reason to believe that the driver was unfit to drive through drink or drugs.

Question 4.9

Constable BROWN has attended the scene of a road traffic collision where a van had collided with a parked and unattended car at the side of the road. The parked car had sustained substantial damage and the driver of the van had made off from the collision. People at the scene stated that they had followed the van for some time and they believed the driver was drunk from the manner of driving they had witnessed. Also, they had seen the driver drinking from cans of lager while driving on the road and throwing empty cans out of the window. Constable BROWN was considering searching the van for evidence that the driver had been drinking, using the power under s. 32 of the Police and Criminal Evidence Act 1984.

> Which of the following statements is correct in relation to any power Constable BROWN may have to search the vehicle in these circumstances?

A Constable BROWN may not search the vehicle under this section; it is restricted to searching for articles which may assist a person to escape from lawful custody.

B Constable BROWN may search the vehicle under this section for anything which might be evidence relating to an offence.

C Constable BROWN may not conduct a search under this section; it is restricted to searching people or premises and not vehicles.

D Constable BROWN may not conduct a search under this section; the driver has not been arrested for an indictable offence.

Question 4.10

A burglary occurred in the early hours of the morning; a witness took the registration number of a vehicle driving away. Following intelligence checks, Constable JULIEN traced the vehicle to BARRY and attended BARRY's home with Constable RUSSELL. Entering the street, the officers saw BARRY stood next to the suspect vehicle, which was parked outside the relevant address. As the officers approached, BARRY was using a mobile phone and they heard him say, 'Get round the house now and get rid of the stuff! The police are here!' Constable RUSSELL immediately arrested BARRY for burglary and the officers debated whether they had a power to enter the premises immediately, to try to prevent any stolen property being disposed of.

Given that the officers were correct in assuming that BARRY lived at the address, could Constable JULIEN enter and search the premises (under s. 18 of the Police and Criminal Evidence Act 1984) without further authority?

A No, Constable JULIEN would require written authority from an inspector to enter and search the premises.

B No, Constable JULIEN would require authority from an inspector, but because of the urgency of the situation this may be verbal; the authority must be confirmed in writing as soon as is reasonably practicable.

C Yes, provided Constable JULIEN had reasonable grounds to believe BARRY was on the premises immediately prior to the arrest.

D Yes, provided Constable JULIEN informed an inspector as soon as practicable after the search was conducted.

Question 4.11

Constable ELLIS attended a dwelling burglary in progress at 2 am. On arrival, the officer was told that the householders had disturbed the suspect, who had escaped through the back door into the rear garden. They had seen the suspect carrying a bag, believed to have contained items stolen from their house. The victims' rear garden was enclosed and was adjacent to several other houses; it was believed that the suspect had climbed over fences and escaped through the other gardens, on to the main street nearby. Whilst making a search of the area, Constable ELLIS received a message that GRAFF had been arrested in a street nearby, by other officers, and that he matched the suspect's description. However, this person was not carrying a bag as described by the witnesses. Constable ELLIS intended returning to the crime scene to search the neighbours' gardens for the bag, to try to link it to GRAFF.

What authority, if any, would Constable ELLIS require, in order to search neighbours' gardens, in these circumstances?

A Constable ELLIS would require the occupiers' permission, unless she was in immediate pursuit of a suspect.

B Constable ELLIS would not require the occupiers' permission, as this may cause disproportionate inconvenience to the person concerned.

C Constable ELLIS would not require the occupiers' permission, as this may cause disproportionate inconvenience to the investigation.

D Constable ELLIS would require the statutory authority of a warrant or through PACE (s. 17, 18 or 32). Otherwise she would require the occupiers' permission.

Question 4.12

Constable ALLEN has attended SAYEED's home address to serve him with a Terrorism Prevention and Investigation Measures (TPIM) notice, under s. 2 of the Terrorism Prevention and Investigation Measures Act 2011, to restrict his movements because of his suspected links to terrorism. The TPIM requires SAYEED to reside at the address on the notice and prohibits him from travelling overseas. The notice also contains a list of people that SAYEED is not to contact. On serving the notice, Constable ALLEN decided that SAYEED's address should be searched to discover anything that might breach any measures specified in the TPIM notice.

Which of the following statements is correct, in relation to whether Constable ALLEN may search SAYEED's address?

A A search of premises in connection with a TPIM notice may only be made under warrant.

B A search of premises may only be made in connection with a TPIM notice without a warrant, where the person has absconded.

C A search of premises may only be made in connection with a TPIM notice without a warrant, if it is conducted for the purposes of finding the individual on whom the notice is to be served.

D A search of premises may be made without a warrant at the time of serving a TPIM notice, to ascertain whether there is anything in the premises that contravenes measures specified in the notice.

ANSWERS

Answer 4.1

Answer **C** — Where police officers enter premises lawfully (including where they are there by invitation), they are on the premises for all lawful purposes (*Foster* v *Attard* [1986] Crim LR 627). This means that they can carry out any lawful functions while on the premises, even if that was not the original purpose for entry. For instance, if officers entered under a lawful power provided by the Misuse of Drugs Act 1971, they may carry out other lawful functions, which would include a general power under s. 19(3) of the Police and Criminal Evidence Act 1984 to seize anything which is on the premises if the officer has reasonable grounds for believing that it is evidence in relation to an offence which he/she is investigating or any other offence and that it is necessary to seize it in order to prevent the evidence being concealed, lost, altered or destroyed.

Answers A, B and D are therefore incorrect.

General Police Duties, para. 4.4.1

Answer 4.2

Answer **B** — Code B, para. 2.9 of the PACE Codes of Practice relating to searches of premises by police officers states:

Nothing in this Code requires the identity of officers, or anyone accompanying them during a search of premises, to be recorded or disclosed:
(a) in the case of enquiries linked to the investigation of terrorism; or
(b) if officers reasonably believe recording or disclosing their names might put them in danger.

Paragraph 2.9 places the decision-making powers in respect of disclosing their identity (when they are investigating specific offences covered in para. 2.9(b)) firmly with the officers—or the people accompanying them—who are conducting the search.

Note for Guidance 2E states that the purpose of para. 2.9(b) is to protect those involved in serious organised crime investigations or arrests of particularly violent suspects when there is reliable information that those arrested or their associates may threaten or cause harm to the officers or anyone accompanying them during a search of premises.

Note for Guidance 2E also states that in cases of doubt, an officer of inspector rank or above should be consulted.

Whilst the search under s. 18 must be authorised by an inspector, there is no specific requirement for him/her to authorise the non-disclosure of the officer's identification in writing prior to the search and answers A and D are incorrect.

Whilst this paragraph does apply to cases linked to the investigation of terrorism, it is not exclusive in respect of non-disclosure of the identification of the officers conducting the search and answer C is incorrect.

General Police Duties, paras 4.4.3, 4.4.3.1

Answer 4.3

Answer **B** — Section 15(2)(iii) of the Police and Criminal Evidence Act 1984 states:

> if the application is for a warrant authorising entry and search on more than one occasion, the ground on which he applies for such a warrant, and whether he seeks a warrant authorising an unlimited number of entries, or (if not) the maximum number of entries desired.

Therefore, an officer will normally be required to specify the number of entries desired and the warrant will *not* automatically authorise unlimited entries. Answer C is therefore incorrect.

On the other hand, s. 15(2)(iii) does provide some flexibility in case the number of entries is unknown (answer A is therefore incorrect).

Section 16(3B) of the Act deals with the authority required from an inspector in relation to multiple entry warrants. Under this section, premises may not be entered or searched for the second or any subsequent time under a warrant which authorises multiple entries, unless a police officer of at least the rank of inspector has authorised that in writing. The section does not give an inspector the power to authorise multiple entries; on the contrary, it places a restriction on such warrants so that each entry must be authorised by an inspector, even when multiple entries have been authorised by a magistrate. Answer D is therefore incorrect.

General Police Duties, paras 4.4.3.2, 4.4.3.3

Answer 4.4

Answer **A** — Section 16 of the Police and Criminal Evidence Act 1984 states:

> (3A) If the warrant is an all premises warrant, no premises which are not specified in it may be entered or searched unless a police officer of at least the rank of inspector has in writing authorised them to be entered.

There is no provision under this section for a senior officer on duty to authorise entry to new premises if an inspector is not readily available and there is no requirement for a superintendent to sign the authorisation. Answers B and D are therefore incorrect.

Also, there will be no requirement for the officer to apply to a magistrate for another all premises warrant to search those premises. Answer C is therefore incorrect.

General Police Duties, para. 4.4.3.3

Answer 4.5

Answer **A** — Section 16(7) of PACE states that if there is no person present who appears to the constable to be in charge of the premises, he/she shall leave a copy of the warrant in a prominent place on the premises. There was a clear breach of the terms of the warrant by DC GOMEZ in this case, which means that any entry and search made under a warrant will be unlawful. Further, a failure to follow the requirements of ss. 15 and 16 of PACE may result in the exclusion of any evidence obtained under the warrant. Answer D is therefore incorrect.

Where officers failed to provide the occupier of the searched premises with a copy of the warrant, they were obliged to return the property seized during the search (*R v Chief Constable of Lancashire, ex parte Parker* [1993] QB 577). As this is a possibility, answer C is incorrect.

Very minor departures from the letter of the warrant will not render any search unlawful (*Attorney-General of Jamaica v Williams* [1998] AC 351); however, *Parker* suggests that failing to provide a copy of the warrant would not be considered a *minor* departure from the requirement to do so under s. 16.

General Police Duties, paras 4.4.3.3, 4.4.3.6

Answer 4.6

Answer **B** — Section 23 of PACE states that 'premises' include any place, and in particular:

(a) any vehicle, vessel, aircraft or hovercraft;
(b) any offshore installation;
(c) any renewable energy installation;
(d) any tent or moveable structure.

Answers A and C are therefore incorrect.

Since 'premises' includes any place, officers are not restricted by the fact that they are not yet aware of the location of the party, and therefore answer D is incorrect.

General Police Duties, para. 4.4.3.4

Answer 4.7

Answer **B** — Section 10(1) of the Police and Criminal Evidence Act 1984 states that subject to subs. (2), 'items subject to legal privilege' means:

(a) communications between a professional legal adviser and his client or any person representing his client made in connection with the giving of legal advice to the client;
(b) communications between a professional legal adviser and his client or any person representing his client or between such an adviser or his client or any such representative and any other person made in connection with or in contemplation of legal proceedings and for the purposes of such proceedings; and
(c) items enclosed with or referred to in such communications and made—
(i) in connection with the giving of legal advice; or
(ii) in connection with or in contemplation of legal proceedings and for the purposes of such proceedings,

when they are in the possession of a person who is entitled to possession of them.

Generally, material which falls within the definition in s. 10(1) is subject to legal privilege, which means that it cannot be searched for or seized. However, items held with the intention of furthering a criminal purpose are no longer subject to this privilege (s. 10(2)). Occasions where this will happen are very rare, but could include instances where a solicitor's firm is the subject of a criminal investigation (*R v Leeds Crown Court, ex parte Switalski* [1991] Crim LR 559). Answer A is therefore incorrect.

Although a warrant cannot authorise a search for legally privileged material, the fact that such material is inadvertently seized in the course of a search authorised by a proper warrant does not render the search unlawful (*HM Customs & Excise, ex parte Popely* [2000] Crim LR 388). Answer C is therefore incorrect.

Possession of a warrant under s. 8 does not authorise police officers to seize *all* material found on the relevant premises to be taken away and 'sifted' somewhere else (*R v Chesterfield Justices, ex parte Bramley* [2000] QB 576). Officers using seize and sift powers will have to be able to show that it was essential (rather than simply convenient or preferable) to do so. Answer D is incorrect.

General Police Duties, paras 4.4.3.7, 4.4.3.8, 4.4.8.7

4. Entry, Search and Seizure

Answer 4.8

Answer **B** — There are several powers to enter premises under s. 17 of the Police and Criminal Evidence Act 1984, including circumstances when the constable has reason to believe that the driver was unfit to drive through drink or drugs. However, under s. 17(1)(c)(iiia), provided the constable has reasonable grounds for believing that the person whom he/she is seeking is on the premises, the constable may enter for the purposes of arresting a person for an offence under s. 163 of the Road Traffic Act 1988 (failure to stop when required to do so by constable in uniform). Answer D is therefore incorrect.

There are powers to enter premises, under s. 6E of the Road Traffic Act 1988, to deal with breathalyser offences, where there are reasonable grounds to believe that the driver had been involved in an accident which involved injury to any person; however, this is not the only power of entry and answer A is incorrect.

Finally, there are further powers under s. 17(d) to recapture a person who is unlawfully at large and whom the officer is pursuing; however, the power to enter premises under s. 17(iiia) does not require the constable to be in 'immediate pursuit' and answer C is incorrect.

General Police Duties, para. 4.4.5.1

Answer 4.9

Answer **D** — Under s. 32(2)(a) of the Police and Criminal Evidence Act 1984, a constable may search an arrested person for anything:

(i) which he might use to assist him to escape from lawful custody; or
(ii) which might be evidence relating to an offence.

Under s. 32(2)(b), if the offence for which he/she has been arrested is an indictable offence, there is a further power to enter and search any premises in which the person was when arrested or immediately before he/she was arrested for evidence relating to the offence.

The section is not restricted to conducting a search for articles which may assist a person to escape from lawful custody; it may also be used to search for evidence of an offence, so answer A is incorrect.

Section 23 of PACE states that for the purpose of the Act, premises includes any vehicle, vessel, aircraft or hovercraft. Answer C is therefore incorrect.

The use of this power is restricted to searching a person or premises *after* they have been arrested for an indictable offence, which means that answer B is incorrect. It is worth noting that because the offence suspected is a summary offence, the officer would not have been able to utilise this search power even if the driver had remained at the scene.

General Police Duties, para. 4.4.5.2

Answer 4.10

Answer **D** — Under s. 18 of the Police and Criminal Evidence Act 1984, a constable may enter and search any premises occupied or controlled by a person who is under arrest for an indictable offence, if he/she has reasonable grounds for suspecting that there is on the premises evidence, other than items subject to legal privilege, that relates:

(a) to that offence; or
(b) to some other indictable offence which is connected with or similar to that offence.

Generally, the power may not be exercised unless an officer of the rank of inspector or above has authorised it in writing.

However, under s. 18(5), a constable may conduct a search under this subsection *before* the person is taken to a police station, without obtaining an authorisation, if the presence of the person at a place (other than a police station) is necessary for the effective investigation of the offence.

The circumstances described in this question would be covered by the exception in s. 18(5) and answers A and B are incorrect.

There is no requirement to show that the defendant was on the premises intended to be searched immediately prior to the arrest. This is a requirement for a search conducted under s. 32 of the Act and does not apply in these circumstances. Answer C is therefore incorrect.

General Police Duties, para. 4.4.5.3

Answer 4.11

Answer **B** — Generally, Code B of the PACE Codes of Practice deals with the search of premises through the statutory authority of a warrant or through PACE (s. 17, 18 or 32). However, para. 5 of this Code deals with searches with the consent of the occupier, or the person 'entitled to grant consent'.

Paragraphs 5.1 to 5.3 deal with how such consent should be obtained; however, para. 5.4 states that it is unnecessary to seek consent if this would cause disproportionate inconvenience *to the person concerned.* Answer C is incorrect, as it is the inconvenience to the occupier that matters.

Note for Guidance 5C outlines that para. 5.4 is intended to apply when it is reasonable to assume innocent occupiers would agree to, and expect, police to take the proposed action, e.g. if:

- a suspect has fled the scene of a crime or to evade arrest and it is necessary quickly to check surrounding gardens and readily accessible places to see if the suspect is hiding;
- police have arrested someone in the night after a pursuit and it is necessary to make a brief check of gardens along the pursuit route to see if stolen or incriminating articles have been discarded.

Therefore, it would be reasonable for Constable ELLIS to search the gardens without the occupiers' permission, even though she was not in immediate pursuit of a suspect, because to have woken the entire street in the middle of the night to search for a bag may have seemed disproportionate in these circumstances. This search could have been conducted *without* the statutory authority of a warrant, or other powers derived from PACE. Answers A and D are therefore incorrect.

General Police Duties, paras 4.4.5, 4.4.6.1

Answer 4.12

Answer **D** — Terrorism Prevention and Investigation Measures (TPIMs) are a civil preventative measure, issued under s. 2 of the Terrorism Prevention and Investigation Measures Act 2011, which are intended to protect the public from the risk posed by suspected terrorists who can be neither prosecuted nor, in the case of foreign nationals, deported, by imposing restrictions intended to prevent or disrupt their engagement in terrorism-related activity.

Section 24 gives effect to sch. 5. The schedule provides for powers of entry, search, seizure and retention in a number of scenarios relating to TPIM notices. These include:

Without a warrant:

- the power to search *without a search warrant in para.* 5 (for purposes of serving TPIM notice), finding the individual on whom the notice is to be served;
- the power to search *without a search warrant in para.* 6 (at time of serving TPIM notice), ascertaining whether there is anything in the premises that contravenes measures specified in the notice;

- the power to search *without a search warrant under para.* 7 (suspected absconding), ascertaining whether a person has absconded or if there is anything on the premises which will assist in the pursuit or arrest of an individual in respect of whom a TPIM notice is in force who is reasonably suspected of having absconded.

With a warrant:

- in relation to the power to search *under a search warrant issued under para.* 8 (for compliance purposes), determining whether an individual in respect of whom a TPIM notice is in force is complying with measures specified in the notice.

Therefore, searches *may* take place without a warrant for several reasons and answers A, B and C are incorrect.

General Police Duties, para. 4.4.11

5 | **Powers of Arrest**

STUDY PREPARATION

This chapter is highly relevant in preparing for the sergeants' or inspectors' examination.

In deciding what to do in any given situation, it is vital that you know what you are *empowered* to do. It is also important to realise that each police power equals a reduction of, or interference with, someone's human rights. As holders of such powers, police officers are under a duty to exercise them properly—lawfully, proportionately and fairly.

An understanding of s. 24 of PACE and Code G of the PACE Codes of Practice is critical for operational officers, in respect of what constitutes a lawful arrest and when an arrest is 'necessary'.

QUESTIONS

Question 5.1

MOSS is taking a case to the European Court of Human Rights, alleging a breach of Art. 5 of the Convention (the right to liberty and security). The circumstances are that SMITH had been arrested for attempting to enter the United Kingdom illegally and had been detained in a temporary centre, pending an application to enter the country as an asylum seeker. MOSS's argument is that his arrest and detention were unnecessary because he had family with strong roots in the United Kingdom and that he was not a flight risk.

What does Art. 5 of the European Convention on Human Rights state about the 'necessity' of such an arrest, in these circumstances?

A The State is not required to demonstrate that an arrest is 'necessary' in these circumstances.

B The State is required to demonstrate that all arrests are 'necessary', even in these circumstances.

C The State is required to demonstrate that all arrests are 'necessary', for the purposes of bringing the person before the competent legal authority.

D The State is required to demonstrate that all arrests are 'necessary', for the purposes of bringing the person before the competent legal authority on reasonable suspicion of having committed an offence.

Question 5.2

Constable SMITH was on foot patrol in a busy town centre. The officer heard observations being passed on the radio for a vehicle and a description of the occupant who was wanted for an offence, but, because of the noise coming from nearby traffic, Constable SMITH did not hear what the offence was. Immediately after hearing the radio message, Constable SMITH saw GALE get out of a vehicle nearby; both GALE and the vehicle matched the description given. The officer approached GALE and fearing that he may run off, told him he was under arrest. However, at the time Constable SMITH could not say what the offence was, or the grounds for the arrest.

Has Constable SMITH acted unlawfully, by failing to inform GALE of the reason and grounds for the arrest?

A No, provided GALE is informed of the grounds for the arrest as soon as practicable.

B Yes, an arrest is unlawful unless the person is informed of the grounds at the time of the arrest.

C Yes, an arrest is unlawful unless the person is informed of the specific offence they are being arrested for, at the time of the arrest.

D No, a constable is not required to give this information if he/she reasonably believes that the person may try to escape before being arrested.

Question 5.3

Constable POTTER was called to a domestic disturbance at the home of HENDERSON and LeBOW. On the officer's arrival, HENDERSON was shouting loudly at LeBOW and making threats. Constable POTTER arrested HENDERSON for a breach of the peace and HENDERSON began struggling violently. Constable POTTER later recorded the facts in a pocket notebook, noting that HENDERSON had not been cautioned at the time of the arrest because of the violent struggle.

Which of the following statements is correct in relation to the requirement to caution a person, according to the PACE Codes of Practice?

A There was a requirement for Constable POTTER to caution HENDERSON because she was not cautioned immediately before the arrest.

B There was no requirement for Constable POTTER to caution HENDERSON at the time of arrest, because she was not being arrested for an offence.

C Constable POTTER was required to caution HENDERSON at the time of arrest, because she was not in the process of escaping from the officer.

D There was no requirement for Constable POTTER to caution HENDERSON at the time of arrest; because of her behaviour, however, the officer was required to caution her as soon as practicable afterwards.

Question 5.4

Constable O'NEIL is being investigated for a misconduct offence of excessive use of force during the arrest of COLLINS. COLLINS sustained a fractured wrist when handcuffs were being applied and has made a complaint of assault against the officer. The Professional Standards Department has submitted a file to the Crown Prosecution Service and is awaiting a charging decision. COLLINS is also considering suing the force for unlawful arrest and unlawful detention.

What would the situation be in relation to COLLINS's arrest, if Constable O'NEIL is found guilty of assault in these circumstances?

A If Constable O'NEIL is found guilty in court of assault, it would automatically render the arrest unlawful.

B If Constable O'NEIL is not charged with assault, but proven at a misconduct hearing to have used excessive force, it would automatically render the arrest unlawful.

C Even if the force used by Constable O'NEIL amounted to an assault and/or misconduct, it would not render an otherwise lawful arrest unlawful.

D Constable O'NEIL would have to be found guilty in court of assault and found to have used excessive force in a misconduct hearing, for the arrest to be declared unlawful.

Question 5.5

Constable HAYWOOD stopped JENNINGS for a motoring offence on a road. The officer conducted a PNC check on the vehicle and discovered it was not registered to JENNINGS. Constable HAYWOOD then tried to obtain personal details, but JENNINGS was acting in a vague and evasive manner which led the officer to consider that an arrest may be necessary, under s. 24(5) of the Police and Criminal Evidence Act 1984.

What does Code G, para. 2.9 of the PACE Codes of Practice state about the steps Constable HAYWOOD should take to make sure JENNINGS understands why the arrest would be necessary?

A Constable HAYWOOD must warn JENNINGS that she will be arrested if she fails to give her name and address and, if practicable, tell her why the arrest is necessary.

B If practicable, Constable HAYWOOD should warn JENNINGS that she will be arrested if she fails to give her name and address; also, if it is practicable, the officer should tell her why the arrest is necessary.

C Constable HAYWOOD is not required to warn JENNINGS that she will be arrested if she fails to give her name and address; however, she should be told, if practicable, why the arrest is necessary.

D Constable HAYWOOD is only required to inform JENNINGS of the grounds for the arrest in these circumstances.

Question 5.6

DOWNEY worked as a security guard in a shopping centre and saw FENTON walking towards the public car park outside. It was clear to DOWNEY that FENTON was drunk from the way she was staggering. DOWNEY saw FENTON approach a car with the keys in her hand and decided to detain her, before she could drive the vehicle. DOWNEY made a 'citizen's arrest' on FENTON (for an offence of being in charge of a mechanically propelled vehicle whilst unfit (contrary to s. 4 of the Road Traffic Act 1988)) as she stood alongside the car and then contacted the police on his mobile phone.

Did DOWNEY have the power to arrest FENTON in these circumstances (under s. 24A of the Police and Criminal Evidence Act 1984)?

A Yes, provided it was not reasonably practicable for a constable to make the arrest instead.

B No, a member of the public only has the power to arrest a person to prevent a person from committing an indictable offence.

C Yes, regardless of whether there was a constable available to make the arrest instead.

D No, a member of the public only has the power to arrest a person when an indictable offence is being committed, or has been committed.

Question 5.7

THORPE was arrested for an assault and following a period of detention was charged, fingerprinted, photographed and had provided a sample of DNA. Following THORPE's conviction in court two months later, it was discovered that an administrative error had occurred and the DNA sample had been lost. This information was forwarded to Inspector MARDEN in the Custody Services Department, with a request that a further DNA sample be obtained from THORPE for the database.

Section 63A of the Police and Criminal Evidence Act 1984 provides a power of arrest without warrant to obtain samples from people in certain circumstances; would the use of this power be suitable in these circumstances?

A Yes, a DNA sample has been taken but it is no longer available.

B No, provided the sample THORPE gave was sufficient for analysis.

C Yes, because THORPE has now been convicted of a recordable offence.

D No, there is no power to take a second sample from someone, when they have previously provided one during the investigation.

Question 5.8

Constable FRENCH, an officer from Police Scotland working from Dumfries Police Station, was pursuing a vehicle which was stolen from the Dumfries and Galloway Divisional area. The vehicle crossed the Scottish border into Cumbria Constabulary's area, in England, where it eventually stopped. Before officers from Cumbria Constabulary arrived at the scene, Constable FRENCH arrested the driver, KELLY.

What action should now be taken, in respect of KELLY?

A KELLY must be taken to the nearest designated station in Scotland, where the original offence took place.

B KELLY must be taken to the nearest designated station in England, where the arrest took place.

C KELLY must be taken to the nearest designated station in Scotland or to the nearest designated police station in England.

D KELLY should be further arrested by an officer from Cumbria Constabulary and be taken to the nearest designated station in England.

Question 5.9

BENTLEY was in police detention waiting to appear in court. He had been arrested for a warrant which had been issued by the court for failing to appear to answer a charge of burglary. BENTLEY asked to see the duty inspector to make a complaint against Constable MOORE, who had arrested him the previous evening. The foundation for BENTLEY's complaint was that Constable MOORE was not in possession of the warrant when she arrested him, and that she did not tell him he was under arrest.

If BENTLEY's case was genuine, has Constable MOORE acted unlawfully in these circumstances?

A Yes, Constable MOORE should have been in possession of the warrant at the time of the arrest and she should have informed BENTLEY that he was under arrest.

B No, there was no requirement for Constable MOORE to have been in possession of the warrant at the time of the arrest, or to have informed BENTLEY that he was under arrest.

C Yes, although there was no requirement for Constable MOORE to have been in possession of the warrant at the time of the arrest, she should have informed BENTLEY that he was under arrest.

D Yes, Constable MOORE should have been in possession of the warrant at the time of the arrest, although it was not necessary for her to inform BENTLEY that he was under arrest.

Question 5.10

DC SHARPE was interviewing HUNTER for a burglary. The officer suspected that HUNTER had committed more than one burglary, but only had reasonable grounds to arrest him for the one offence. In the interview, HUNTER provided DC SHARPE with reasonable grounds to suspect he should be arrested for two other offences. At that time, the officer made a decision that HUNTER would be further arrested for those offences, but not until after the interview. HUNTER was actually arrested for the further offences two hours after the interview concluded.

Considering s. 31 of the Police and Criminal Evidence Act 1984, which of the following statements is correct in relation to the timing of HUNTER's arrest?

A HUNTER should have been arrested when DC SHARPE had reasonable grounds to suspect him of further offences; the officer has acted unlawfully.

B HUNTER should have been arrested when DC SHARPE made the decision to arrest him for the further offences; the officer has acted unlawfully.

C HUNTER should have been arrested before the end of the interview; the officer has acted unlawfully.

D DC SHARPE has acted lawfully; there was no requirement to arrest HUNTER before the officer did so.

Question 5.11

MILLS had been detained by Constable GROVES for an offence of burglary which occurred an hour ago. MILLS matched the description of a person seen running away from the scene; the officer informed him he was under arrest and after caution, MILLS replied, 'It couldn't have been me, I was in my mate's house. Take me round there now and he'll tell you I was there.'

Section 30(1A) of the Police and Criminal Evidence Act 1984 requires a person to be taken by a constable to a police station as soon as practicable after the arrest. Would the information provided by MILLS allow Constable GROVES to deviate to his friend's address before taking him to the station?

A Yes, this may be a valid reason for not taking a person to a police station as soon as practicable after the arrest, provided the matter required immediate investigation.

B No, the only reason not to take a person to a police station as soon as practicable after the arrest is to recover evidence related to an indictable offence for which he/she has been arrested.

C No, a person must be taken to a police station as soon as practicable after the arrest on every occasion.

D No, there are circumstances in which a person may not be taken to a police station as soon as practicable after the arrest; however, checking an alibi would not amount to such an exception.

Question 5.12

VIZARD has been working for a charity organisation as a healthcare worker based in Monrovia (Liberia) for the past five years. On a Christmas break, VIZARD returns to her home in London but several days after arriving home she begins to feel extremely unwell and visits a hospital. At the hospital, she is examined and diagnosed with Ebola virus disease (an extremely infectious and dangerous condition). Due to the nature of the disease, there is extreme concern about the spread of the disease as well as concern for the health of VIZARD.

Can VIZARD be detained under Art. 5 of the European Convention on Human Rights?

A No, as Art. 5 does not provide any power to arrest or detain; it simply sets out certain circumstances where the general right to liberty may be interfered with by some existing lawful means.

B Yes, as Art. 5 provides a power of detention when it is necessary and proportionate to deprive a person of their liberty in order to prevent the spread of infectious diseases.

C No, as Art. 5 would not be applicable to this situation as whilst it provides numerous powers to arrest (if the arrest is for a lawful and legitimate reason), it does not address issues connected to the continued detention of an individual.

D Yes, if it could be shown that releasing VIZARD from the hospital would be likely to be detrimental to public health.

Question 5.13

PC BABBINGTON is a probationary constable and is on patrol with PS RABY (an experienced police officer with 20 years' service). PC BABBINGTON is struggling to grasp some of the concepts in respect of the information that is required to be given to a suspect when they are arrested. PC BABBINGTON makes several comments about the information required but only one is correct.

Which of the following comments by PC BABBINGTON shows a correct understanding of the law?

A Section 28 of the Police and Criminal Evidence Act 1984 states that when a person is arrested using the powers under the Police and Criminal Evidence Act 1984 they must be told they are under arrest and given the grounds for the arrest unless it is not practicable to do so. These requirements do not have to be satisfied when arresting a person using other powers.

B When a person is arrested by a constable and it is obvious to that person that they have been arrested, the constable does not actually have to tell that person that they have been arrested.

C A failure by a police officer to comply with the requirements of s. 28 of the Police and Criminal Evidence Act 1984 will not make the arrest unlawful.

D The requirement to indicate to a person the fact that they have been arrested might be met by using a colloquialism, such as 'You're nicked' or 'You're locked up', providing the person understands its meaning.

ANSWERS

Answer 5.1

Answer **A** — Article 5(1) of the European Convention on Human Rights states:

> Everyone has the right to liberty and security of person. No one shall be deprived of his liberty save in the following cases and in accordance with a procedure prescribed by law.

Under Art. 5(1)(c), it must be demonstrated that the arrest or detention of a person was effected for the purpose of bringing him/her before the competent legal authority on reasonable suspicion of having committed an offence or when it is reasonably considered necessary to prevent him/her committing an offence or fleeing after having done so.

However, other subsections in Art. 5 do not require the arrest to be made for the purpose of bringing the person before the competent legal authority. Under Art. 5(1)(f), the lawful arrest or detention of a person may be made:

> to prevent his effecting an unauthorised entry into the country or of a person against whom action is being taken with a view to deportation or extradition.

Answers C and D are therefore incorrect.

In the case of *R (On the Application of Saadi)* v *Secretary of State for the Home Department* [2002] UKHL 41, the House of Lords ruled that, unlike part of Art. 5(1)(c), Art. 5(1)(f) does *not* require that detention has to be necessary in order to be justified. As a result, the temporary detention of asylum seekers, pending their application to remain in the United Kingdom, is not of itself unlawful. Answer B is therefore incorrect.

General Police Duties, para. 4.5.2

Answer 5.2

Answer **A** — Section 28(1) and (3) of the Police and Criminal Evidence Act 1984 states:

> Subject to subsection (5) below, where a person is arrested, otherwise than by being informed that he is under arrest, the arrest is not lawful unless the person arrested is informed that he is under arrest as soon as is practicable after his arrest.
> ...
> Subject to subsection (5) below, no arrest is lawful unless the person arrested is informed of the ground for the arrest at the time of, or as soon as is practicable after, the arrest.

Nothing in s. 28 states that the person must be informed of the specific offence they are being arrested for; the section requires the person to be informed that they are under arrest and the *grounds* for that arrest and the court has held that it does not matter that the words describe more than one offence (e.g. 'burglary' or 'fraud'), provided that they adequately describe the offence for which the person has been arrested (*Abbassy* v *Metropolitan Police Commissioner* [1990] 1 WLR 385). Answer C is therefore incorrect.

The officer has complied with s. 28(1), in the previous extract, by informing the person he is under arrest; subs. (3), in the previous extract, allows for a person to be told the information as soon as is practicable after the arrest, which in this case could be when the officer manages to speak to a colleague or the control room over the radio. Answer B is therefore incorrect.

Finally, s. 28(5) states that nothing in this section is to be taken to require a person to be informed:

(a) that he is under arrest; or
(b) of the ground for the arrest,

if it was not reasonably practicable for him to be so informed by reason of his having escaped from arrest before the information could be given.

However, there is no provision for the officer to fail to give the information if he/she reasonably believes that the person may try to escape before being arrested and answer D is therefore incorrect.

General Police Duties, para. 4.5.3.1

Answer 5.3

Answer **B** — Code C, para. 10.4 of the PACE Codes of Practice requires that a person must be cautioned on arrest or further arrest. There are exceptions to the requirement to administer the caution and these are:

- where it is impracticable to do so by reason of the person's condition or behaviour at the time; or
- where he/she has already been cautioned immediately before the arrest in accordance with Code C, para. 10.1 (requirement to caution where there are grounds to suspect commission of an offence).

However, consideration also needs to be given to Code G, para. 4, Note for Guidance 1A, which states that the Code will not apply where a person is being arrested for a warrant or other matters, such as a breach of bail. It also states that the Code does not apply when a person is being arrested under a common law power to stop or prevent a breach of the peace. The caution should be given if it is intended to question a person about an 'offence' and since this is not a requirement for an arrest which is meant to simply place a person before the court, a caution is not required regardless of any other exceptions in Code C. Answers A and C are therefore incorrect.

Section 28(5) of PACE allows that a person need not be informed of the reason or grounds for their arrest if it was not reasonably practicable by reason of his/her having escaped from arrest before the information could be given. However, this exception is not listed in Code C, para. 10.4, which relates to cautions. Answer C is incorrect for this reason also.

There is nothing in Code C requiring a person to be cautioned as soon as practicable after their arrest, if they were not cautioned at the time, and therefore answer D is incorrect.

General Police Duties, paras 4.5.3.1, 4.5.3.2

Answer 5.4

Answer **C** — Section 117 of the Police and Criminal Evidence Act 1984 allows the use of reasonable force when making an arrest. Section 3 of the Criminal Law Act 1967 also allows the use of such force as is reasonably necessary in the arrest of people and the prevention of crime.

For an arrest to be lawful, it must be 'necessary' under s. 24 of the Police and Criminal Evidence Act 1984 and this is the test that a court would apply. The use of excessive force, while amounting to possible misconduct and assault, does not render an otherwise lawful arrest unlawful (*Simpson* v *Chief Constable of South Yorkshire* (1991) 135 SJ 383).

Answers A, B and D are therefore incorrect.

General Police Duties, para. 4.5.3.3

Answer 5.5

Answer **B** — Code G, para. 2.9 of the PACE Codes of Practice states:

When it is practicable to tell a person why their arrest is necessary (as required by paragraphs 2.2 and 3.3), the constable should outline the facts, information and other circumstances which provide the grounds for believing that their arrest is necessary and which the officer considers satisfy one or more of the statutory criteria in sub-paragraphs (a) to (f).

Answer D is therefore incorrect.

A warning is not expressly required by para. 2.9, but officers should, if practicable, consider whether to issue a warning which points out the person's offending behaviour, and explains why, if the person does not stop, the resulting consequences may make his/her arrest necessary. Such a warning might:

- if heeded, avoid the need to arrest; or
- if ignored, support the need to arrest and also help prove the mental element of certain offences, for example the person's intent or awareness, or help to rebut a defence that he/she was acting reasonably.

Answers A and C are incorrect for this reason.

General Police Duties, paras 4.5.5.4, 4.5.5.6

Answer 5.6

Answer **D** — Under s. 24A of the Police and Criminal Evidence Act 1984 certain powers of arrest are provided for any person. Section 24A states:

(1) A person other than a constable may arrest without a warrant—
  (a) anyone who is in the act of committing an indictable offence;
  (b) anyone whom he has reasonable grounds for suspecting to be committing an indictable offence.
(2) Where an indictable offence has been committed, a person other than a constable may arrest without a warrant—
  (a) anyone who is guilty of the offence;
  (b) anyone whom he has reasonable grounds for suspecting to be guilty of it.
(3) But the power of summary arrest conferred by subsection (1) or (2) is exercisable only if—
  (a) the person making the arrest has reasonable grounds for believing that for any of the reasons mentioned in subsection (4) it is necessary to arrest the person in question; and
  (b) it appears to the person making the arrest that it is not reasonably practicable for a constable to make it instead.
(4) The reasons are to prevent the person in question—
  (a) causing physical injury to himself or any other person;
  (b) suffering physical injury;
  (c) causing loss of or damage to property; or
  (d) making off before a constable can assume responsibility for him.

Section 24A(4)(d) of PACE does allow a member of the public to make a 'citizen's' arrest, where it is not reasonably practicable for a constable to make it instead;

however, unlike the powers of arrest available to police officers (which apply to all offences), the 'citizen's' power of arrest only applies where the relevant offence is *indictable*. An offence under s. 4 of the Road Traffic Act 1988 is a summary only offence. Answers A and C are therefore incorrect.

Under s. 24A, a person other than a constable may make such an arrest when an indictable offence *is* being committed, or *has* been committed; the power to make a preventative arrest (i.e. where an indictable offence is *about* to be committed) only applies to police officers. Answer B is therefore incorrect.

General Police Duties, para. 4.5.8

Answer 5.7

Answer **B** — Section 63A of the Police and Criminal Evidence Act 1984 provides a power of arrest without warrant in respect of people who:

- have been charged with/reported for a recordable offence and who have not had a sample taken or the sample was unsuitable/insufficient for analysis;
- have been convicted of a recordable offence and have not had a sample taken since conviction;
- have been so convicted and have had a sample taken before or since conviction but the sample was unsuitable/insufficient for analysis.

Whether the person has been charged or convicted, the only reason to arrest them to take samples is when the sample has not previously been taken or, if it has been taken, it was insufficient for analysis; however, a sample may not be taken simply because it has been lost by the police. Answers A and C are incorrect.

Answer D is incorrect because there *is* a power to take a second sample from someone, when they have previously provided one during the investigation, but it cannot be done in the circumstances described.

General Police Duties, para. 4.5.9.4

Answer 5.8

Answer **C** — The Criminal Justice and Public Order Act 1994 (ss. 136 to 140) makes provision for officers from one part of the United Kingdom to go into another part of the United Kingdom to arrest someone there in connection with an offence committed within their jurisdiction, and gives them powers to search on arrest.

A Scottish police officer may arrest someone suspected of committing an offence in Scotland who is found in England, Wales or Northern Ireland if it would have been lawful to arrest that person had he/she been found in Scotland. Since this power is granted to Constable FRENCH, there is no requirement for an officer from an English police force to further arrest KELLY and therefore answer D is incorrect.

Where an officer from a Scottish police force has arrested someone suspected of committing an offence in Scotland, who is found in England, the officer must take the person to the nearest convenient designated police station in Scotland *or* to the nearest convenient designated police station in England or Wales (see s. 137(7)).

Section 137(7) goes on to say that the person must be taken to the police station as soon as reasonably practicable. This would suggest that the arrested person should be taken to the nearest police station if the distance to one or another is too great. Since the arresting officer has a choice of police stations, answers A and B are incorrect.

General Police Duties, para. 4.5.9.5

Answer 5.9

Answer **C** — Warrants issued in connection with 'an offence' do not need to be in the possession of the officer executing them at the time. Answers A and D are therefore incorrect.

However, the requirement under s. 28 of the Police and Criminal Evidence Act 1984, to tell a person why he/she is being arrested, *does* apply to arrests under warrant. Answers B and D are incorrect for this reason also.

General Police Duties, para. 4.5.10

Answer 5.10

Answer **D** — Section 31 of the Police and Criminal Evidence Act 1984 states that where:

(a) a person—
    (i) has been arrested for an offence; and
    (ii) is at a police station in consequence of that arrest; and
(b) it appears to a constable that, if he were released from that arrest, he would be liable to arrest for some other offence, he shall be arrested for that other offence.

In *R v Samuel* [1988] QB 615, the Court of Appeal said that the purpose of the s. 31 requirement was to prevent the release and immediate re-arrest of an offender—therefore, the court noted, s. 31 did not prevent any further arrest from being delayed until the release of the prisoner for the initial arrest was imminent.

Therefore, there was no requirement to arrest HUNTER at any time before he was actually arrested. The only obligation under s. 31 is that the person should not be released from police detention and then rearrested, when there were sufficient grounds to arrest him/her before he/she was released. Answers A, B and C are therefore incorrect.

General Police Duties, para. 4.5.11

Answer 5.11

Answer **A** — Section 30 of the Police and Criminal Evidence Act 1984 states:

(1) Subsection (1A) applies where a person is, at any place other than a police station—
   (a) arrested by a constable for an offence, or
   (b) taken into custody by a constable after being arrested for an offence by a person other than a constable.
(1A) The person must be taken by a constable to a police station as soon as practicable after the arrest.

Section 30(1A) allows the officer to delay taking the arrested person to a police station where his/her presence elsewhere is necessary in order to carry out such investigations as it is reasonable to carry out immediately. Where there is such a delay, the reasons for it must be recorded when the person first arrives at the police station (s. 30(11)). Section 30(10) was confirmed in *R* v *Kerawalla* [1991] Crim LR 451, where the court held that if the matter can wait, the exception will not apply and the person must be taken straight to a police station. Answer C is therefore incorrect.

In *Dallison* v *Caffery* [1965] 1 QB 348, it was held that taking an arrested person to check out an alibi before going to a police station *may* be justified in some circumstances. Answer D is therefore incorrect.

Section 18(5)(a) of the Act allows a premises to be searched before the person is taken to a police station for evidence related to an indictable offence for which the person has been arrested or some other indictable offence which is connected with or similar to that offence. However, this is an *additional* power to the one under s. 30(10) and answer B is incorrect.

General Police Duties, paras 4.5.12, 4.3.5.1, 4.3.5.3

Answer 5.12

Answer **A** — A person may be deprived of their liberty for a number of legitimate and lawful reasons.

Article 5 of the Convention states:

1. Everyone has the right to liberty and security of person. No one shall be deprived of his liberty save in the following cases and in accordance with a procedure prescribed by law:
    (a) the lawful detention of a person after conviction by a competent court;
    (b) the lawful arrest or detention of a person for non-compliance with the lawful order of a court or in order to secure the fulfilment of any obligation prescribed by law;
    (c) the lawful arrest or detention of a person effected for the purpose of bringing him before the competent legal authority on reasonable suspicion of having committed an offence or when it is reasonably considered necessary to prevent his committing an offence or fleeing after having done so;
    (d) the detention of a minor by lawful order for the purpose of educational supervision or his lawful detention for the purpose of bringing him before the competent legal authority;
    (e) the lawful detention of persons for the prevention of the spreading of infectious diseases, of persons of unsound mind, alcoholics or drug addicts or vagrants;
    (f) the lawful arrest or detention of a person to prevent his effecting an unauthorised entry into the country or of a person against whom action is being taken with a view to deportation or extradition.

A person can only be deprived of his/her general right to liberty under one of the conditions set out on the permitted grounds in Art. 5(1)(a)–(f), and even then that deprivation must be carried out in accordance with a *procedure prescribed by law*. Article 5 does not provide a power of arrest or detention, making answers B, C and D incorrect. Article 5 relates to a multitude of situations where an individual has been arrested or detained but does not provide any power to arrest or detain; it simply sets out certain circumstances where the general right to liberty may be interfered with by some existing lawful means. Whatever its extent, Art. 5(1)(e) is likely to be narrowly applied by the courts and the mere fact that an individual has, for example, an infectious disease, will not of itself justify his/her 'detention'.

General Police Duties, para. 4.5.2

Answer 5.13

Answer **D** — Answer A is incorrect as whether an arrest is made under the Police and Criminal Evidence Act 1984 *or not*, s. 28 of the Act makes it clear that the person must be told they are being arrested and the grounds for the arrest. The requirement for a person to be informed that they are under arrest applies regardless of whether the fact of the arrest is obvious, making answer B incorrect. A failure to comply with s. 28 will make an arrest unlawful (see e.g. *Dawes* v *DPP* [1994] Crim LR 604), making answer C incorrect.

General Police Duties, para. 4.5.3.1

6 Hatred and Harassment Offences

STUDY PREPARATION

The law in relation to offences involving hatred and harassment is wide-ranging and provides offences and powers that enable appropriate action to be taken in relation to such activity and, in certain circumstances, to protect against such activity occurring in the first place.

Covered in this chapter are the powers given to the police and the courts to deal with personal harassment and stalking, which are covered in various pieces of legislation such as the Protection from Harassment Act 1997 and the Public Order Act 1986.

QUESTIONS

Question 6.1

MEREDITH holds racist opinions about black people. One day he was at home with several friends who share his beliefs, when COWANS, who is black, knocked on his door collecting money on behalf of charity. MEREDITH invited COWANS into his house on the pretext of looking for money. When they were in the living room of the house, MEREDITH began racially abusing COWANS in front of his friends. His intention all along was to stir up racial hatred. When COWANS eventually left the house, he contacted the police to report the incident.

Considering offences under s. 18 of the Public Order Act 1986 (using words or behaviour or displaying written material stirring up racial hatred), does the fact that the incident took place in a dwelling affect whether or not the police can take any action?

A No, the offence may be committed anywhere.

B Yes, the offence may only be committed in a public place.

C No, the offence may be committed in a public or private place.

D Yes, the offence may not be committed when both persons are in a dwelling.

Question 6.2

WADE lives in a small cul-de-sac and is openly homophobic. WADE became aware that two people of the same sex had bought a house in the street and the rumours amongst the neighbours were that the people were in a homosexual relationship. One day, neighbours noticed several posters in the front windows of WADE's house, on which were written, 'Sign my petition to get rid of sexual deviants from this street'. WADE's intention was to make the new neighbours uncomfortable about living in the area, so that they would move out.

Could WADE be guilty of an offence under s. 29B of the Public Order Act 1986, of stirring up hatred against the neighbours, on the grounds of sexual orientation?

A No, WADE has not made threats to the neighbours, intending to stir up hatred on the grounds of their sexual orientation.

B Yes, WADE has used threatening, abusive or insulting words or behaviour, about a person's sexual orientation.

C No, this offence can only be committed where a person uses words or behaviour, and does not include the use of written materials.

D Yes, WADE has used threatening, abusive or insulting words or behaviour, intending to stir up hatred on the grounds of sexual orientation, or where hatred was likely to be stirred up.

Question 6.3

CRUTCHER and BOYCE are members of an animal rights extremist group and were targeting two companies, which CRUTCHER and BOYCE believed were suppliers to a third company which tested its products on animals. Following a discussion between the two, CRUTCHER sent a threatening letter to the chief executive of one company supplying the goods and BOYCE sent a threatening email to the chief executive of the other company supplying the goods. Their intention was to persuade both companies to stop supplying the third company with their products.

Given that the recipients are likely to be caused alarm and distress by the communications, would CRUTCHER and BOYCE's actions amount to a 'course of conduct' in respect of an offence under s. 1(1A) of the Protection from Harassment Act 1997?

A Yes, their conduct would be sufficient to amount to a 'course of conduct' in these circumstances.

B No, each person would have to send communications to at least two people.

C No, each person would have to send communications to at least two people from each company.

D No, because the communication they sent to each person was in a different form.

Question 6.4

REEVES has sent two threatening letters to his probation officer. However, the second letter was not received until four-and-a-half months after the first.

Could REEVES be guilty of harassment contrary to ss. 1 and 2 of the Protection from Harassment Act 1997?

A No, as probation officers are unlikely to feel distress.

B No, owing to the length of time between the letters.

C Yes, but only if the probation officer is likely to feel alarmed and distressed.

D Yes, but only if the probation officer is likely to feel alarmed or distressed.

Question 6.5

Following the break-up of a long-term relationship with FRAMPTON, CLARKSON moved away to live with friends in Scotland. Before leaving, CLARKSON was convicted of harassment against FRAMPTON, contrary to s. 2 of the Protection from Harassment Act 1997. FRAMPTON has heard that CLARKSON intends returning to live nearby and has also been told by friends that CLARKSON is still angry about the break-up and will try to resume contact. FRAMPTON intends seeking a county court injunction against CLARKSON, to avoid being subjected to further harassment.

Could a county court issue an injunction in such circumstances, when there has been no evidence that CLARKSON has actually committed a further offence contrary to the Protection from Harassment Act 1997?

A No, only the High Court may issue an injunction in respect of an apprehended breach of the 1997 Act.

B No, an injunction may not be issued in respect of an apprehended breach of the 1997 Act.

C No, an injunction could only be issued in these circumstances if CLARKSON had previously been convicted of an offence contrary to s. 4 of the 1997 Act.

D Yes, the county court could issue an injunction even for an apprehended breach of the 1997 Act.

Question 6.6

MURRAY had been involved in a long-standing dispute with her neighbour, WALTON, and had been made subject to a restraining order under s. 5(1) of the Protection from Harassment Act 1997. The order prohibited MURRAY from 'using abusive words or actions' towards WALTON. While the order was still in force, WALTON was visited by friends, who parked their car in the street outside the house. A short while later, WALTON observed MURRAY move her own car, which was also parked in the street, into such a position that it effectively blocked in WALTON's friends' car. WALTON contacted the police, claiming that MURRAY had breached the restraining order. When the officers arrived, MURRAY claimed that she was not aware that her behaviour amounted to a breach of the order.

Which of the following statements is correct, in respect of whether MURRAY could be found guilty of breaching the restraining order?

A MURRAY's behaviour was not serious enough to amount to harassment; therefore, the restraining order has not been breached.

B MURRAY's behaviour may have amounted to harassment, but she may have a defence if she could show that she honestly believed that her conduct did not breach the terms of the restraining order.

C MURRAY's belief is irrelevant. Once the prosecution demonstrates that the restraining order was in place and the behaviour amounted to harassment, the court should find that the order has been breached.

D MURRAY's behaviour was not directed at WALTON; therefore, the restraining order has not been breached.

Question 6.7

OLTON has been arrested for an offence of harassment, under s. 4 of the Protection from Harassment Act 1997, over a dispute about money owed to him by LOVE. It is alleged that OLTON made three phone calls to LOVE, during which he threatened to injure his family if the money was not paid within a week. OLTON intended LOVE to fear that he would carry out the threat and was prepared to do so.

Given that OLTON has engaged in a course of conduct, what would have to be shown in relation to LOVE's state of mind, in order for the offence to be complete?

A That OLTON's course of conduct caused LOVE to fear that violence would be used against him.

B That OLTON's course of conduct caused LOVE to fear that violence may be used against him.

C That OLTON's course of conduct caused LOVE to fear that violence would be used against him or his family.

D That OLTON's course of conduct caused LOVE to fear that immediate violence would be used against him.

Question 6.8

BERTRAND worked in the Information Department of a police force and specialised in computer programming. BERTRAND had previously been in a relationship with ROSS, a work colleague, which had ended recently. BERTRAND was upset at the break-up and became convinced that ROSS was now in a relationship with another colleague. BERTRAND managed to access ROSS's emails and monitored them remotely every day for about a month, to obtain information about the new relationship. ROSS suspected this was happening and asked BERTRAND to stop. BERTRAND was aware that ROSS was upset, but carried on accessing the emails.

Would BERTRAND's behaviour amount to stalking, under s. 2A(1) of the Protection from Harassment Act 1997?

A Yes, provided a course of conduct can be proved.

B No, this offence requires some positive action by the defendant and BERTRAND has not actually used the information for anything.

C Yes, regardless of whether a course of conduct can be proved.

D No, this offence requires some form of act or omission by the defendant, which has not occurred in these circumstances.

Question 6.9

When BERRY split up from her boyfriend, TROTT, he began posting abusive messages on his Facebook account, calling her a 'slut' and 'whore'. The abuse got worse and TROTT posted a number of photographs on his account of BERRY with no clothes on. Eventually, TROTT posted explicit photographs of the pair having sex. After each Facebook message or photograph, TROTT sent BERRY a message telling her to look at this account. BERRY was not concerned about her safety and initially ignored the abuse and photographs of her with no clothes on; however, she became extremely distressed because of the explicit photographs. Eventually, BERRY moved away from the area and changed her telephone number to avoid receiving messages from TROTT. She also stopped all contact with her family and friends because of the Facebook account.

Would TROTT's behaviour amount to stalking, under s. 4A of the Protection from Harassment Act 1997?

A No, TROTT has not threatened BERRY with violence.

B No, BERRY was not in fear that TROTT would use violence against her.

C No, BERRY only became extremely distressed when TROTT posted the explicit photographs; this was a single act and did not amount to a course of conduct.

D Yes, TROTT has pursued a course of conduct which has had a substantial adverse effect on BERRY's day-to-day activities.

Question 6.10

DONOVAN works in a laboratory where a number of experiments are carried out in relation to genetically modified crops. WARBRICK is opposed to the use and sale of genetically modified crops and follows DONOVAN home from the laboratory one evening. DONOVAN is inside her house when she sees WARBRICK standing on the pavement outside her house holding a sign with 'You are Murdering the Future of Our Children!' written on it. WARBRICK is also repeatedly shouting 'Stop going to work! Stop playing God!' DONOVAN contacts the police and states how distressed she is and, as a result, PS PURCELL and PC TANSILL (on uniform mobile patrol) arrive at the scene. PS PURCELL speaks to WARBRICK who states he only wants DONOVAN to stop her 'evil work', causing PS PURCELL to believe WARBRICK is at the house to persuade DONOVAN that she should not do something that she is entitled to do.

Could a direction under s. 42 of the Criminal Justice and Police Act 2001 be given to WARBRICK in these circumstances?

A Yes, the direction can be given to WARBRICK by PS PURCELL or PC TANSILL.

B No, a direction under s. 42 must be given by an officer of the rank of inspector or above.

C Yes, but the direction must be given to WARBRICK by PS PURCELL.

D No, a direction under s. 42 must be given by an officer of the rank of superintendent or above.

Question 6.11

LITTLEWOOD, RYAN and PERCY are peacefully protesting outside the offices of a financial institution which has business links to Saudi Arabia. The three are protesting about alleged human rights violations in Saudi Arabia and are trying to persuade the workers at the financial institution not to go into work. Inspector HOWSON attends the scene with PC SNETHAM (both officers are on uniform patrol) where they speak to a supervisor at the financial institution. Whilst there have been no allegations that what LITTLEWOOD, RYAN and PERCY are doing involves any unlawful activity, several members of staff at the financial institution have told their supervisor that a number of their clients have cancelled business appointments that day because they had seen the protest reported on a local TV station and consequently the financial institution is losing money.

Is it possible for Inspector HOWSON to give the three protesters a direction to leave the vicinity of the financial institution (using the discretionary power under s. 42 of the Criminal Justice and Police Act 2001)?

A No, because there are no reports that the protesters have caused any workers at the financial institution any harassment, alarm or distress.

B Yes, but this is only possible because Inspector HOWSON is in uniform.

C No, because the power is only available when the person(s) concerned is/are outside (or in the vicinity of) any premises that are used by any individual as his/her dwelling.

D Yes, but any direction given to the protesters must be given in writing.

Question 6.12

LEACH believes that all Muslims are a deadly threat to national security and that they should be forcibly removed from the United Kingdom. Intending to stir up religious hatred, he writes a pamphlet titled 'Muslim Menace' in which he expresses his views on the subject in a very threatening manner. LEACH approaches BRYANT, a publisher, and asks him to publish 1,000 copies of the pamphlet. BRYANT reads the pamphlet and agrees to publish it as he is sympathetic to LEACH's views and also wishes to stir up religious hatred. Once the copies have been made, LEACH picks them up and takes them back to his house. LEACH then asks his friend, PERRY, to stand on a street corner and hand out the pamphlets. PERRY asks what is in the pamphlets as he cannot read. LEACH states that they are in protest about the closure of a local factory and the resulting lost jobs. PERRY agrees to hand out the leaflets and goes out and distributes them to the public on a street near LEACH's house.

Only taking into account the offence of publishing or distributing written material (under s. 29C of the Public Order Act 1986), which of the following comments is true?

A LEACH, BRYANT and PERRY have all committed the offence in these circumstances.

B Only BRYANT has committed the offence in these circumstances.

C Only BRYANT and PERRY commit the offence in these circumstances.

D The offence is not committed in these circumstances.

ANSWERS

Answer 6.1

Answer **D** — An offence is committed contrary to s. 18(1) of the Public Order Act 1986, where a person uses threatening, abusive or insulting words or behaviour, intending to stir up racial hatred (or where it is likely to be stirred up). Certainly, the behaviour of the person in the question would meet these criteria. However, s. 18(2) states that the offence may be committed in a public or private place, but not when the words or behaviour used are not heard by persons other than those in that or another dwelling. The requirement is similar to those under ss. 4 and 5 of the same Act, and since both persons were in the same dwelling, no offence is committed, whatever MEREDITH's intentions! Answers A, B and C are incorrect for this reason.

General Police Duties, para. 4.6.2.1

Answer 6.2

Answer **A** — Section 29B of the 1986 Act defines 'hatred on the grounds of sexual orientation'. The definition covers hatred against a group of persons defined by reference to their sexual orientation, be they heterosexual, homosexual or bisexual. The offence may involve the use of words or behaviour or *display of written material* (s. 29B). Therefore, answer C is incorrect.

However, the offences differ from the offences of stirring up racial hatred in two respects. First, the offences apply only to 'threatening' words or behaviour, rather than 'threatening, abusive or insulting' words or behaviour. The second difference is that in this section, the offences apply only to words or behaviour if the accused 'intends' to stir up hatred on grounds of sexual orientation. They do not apply in circumstances where a person displays a sign about an individual's sexual orientation that is threatening, abusive or insulting or which is 'likely' to stir up hatred without the relevant intention so answers B and D are incorrect.

General Police Duties, para. 4.6.2, 4.6.2.5

Answer 6.3

Answer **A** — Under s. 1(1A) of the Protection from Harassment Act 1997, a person commits an offence if he/she pursues a course of conduct which involves harassment of two or more persons and which he/she knows or ought to know involves harassment of those persons and by which he/she intends to persuade any person not to do something which he/she is entitled or required to do, or to do something that he/she is not under any obligation to do.

Under s. 7(3)(b) of the Act, a course of conduct for this offence must involve, in the case of conduct in relation to two or more people, conduct on at least one occasion to each of those people. The fact that the letters were sent by two different people is irrelevant, because under s. 7(3A), a person's conduct may be aided and abetted by another, and both would commit this offence provided it can be shown they were acting together. Answer B is therefore incorrect.

Home Office Circular 34/2005 provides examples of offences which might be committed under s. 1(1A). In this guidance, it cites the example of an animal rights extremist sending a threatening email to an individual on one occasion working for one company and another similar letter to a different individual working for another company, with the intention of persuading them to stop supplying a third company with their products (similar to the circumstances in this question). Since the offence may be committed by sending different forms of communication to only one person from each company, answers C and D are incorrect (this is true even though the communications were sent by two different people).

General Police Duties, para. 4.6.4.4

Answer 6.4

Answer **D** — Section 1 of the Protection from Harassment Act 1997 states that a person must not pursue a course of conduct:

(a) which amounts to harassment of another, and
(b) which he knows or ought to know amounts to harassment of the other.

Course of conduct has been considered by the courts. In *Lau* v *DPP* [2000] 1 FLR 799, the Divisional Court held that although only two incidents are necessary, the fewer the number of incidents and the further apart they are, the less likely it is that there will be a finding of harassment. In *Baron* v *CPS* (2000) 13 June, unreported, the court accepted that the more spread out and limited in number the incidents and the more indirect their means of delivery (in this case by letter), the less likely it is that a course of conduct amounting to harassment will be found. However, there is no rule and it will depend upon the facts of each individual case. In *Baron*, two letters sent some four-and-a-half months apart could be a course of conduct amounting to harassment, and therefore answer B is incorrect.

Note it is alarm *or* distress; the court need only be satisfied that the behaviour involved one or the other (*DPP* v *Ramsdale* [2001] EWHC 106 (Admin)), and therefore answer C is incorrect.

Finally, the court in *Baron* refused to endorse the view that public service employees are less likely to be caused distress by threatening letters, and therefore answer A is incorrect.

General Police Duties, paras 4.6.4.3, 4.6.4.5

Answer 6.5

Answer **D** — Under ss. 3 and 3A of the Protection from Harassment Act 1997, the High Court *or* a county court may issue an injunction in respect of civil proceedings brought in respect of an actual *or* apprehended breach of s. 1(1) and (1A). Answers A and B are therefore incorrect.

The effect of this is that a defendant may be made the subject of an injunction even though their behaviour has not amounted to an offence under the 1997 Act, or regardless of whether they were previously convicted of a s. 4 offence. Answer C is therefore incorrect.

General Police Duties, para. 4.6.4.10

Answer 6.6

Answer **B** — Section 5(5) of the Protection from Harassment Act 1997 states that if without reasonable excuse the defendant does anything which he/she is prohibited from doing by an order under this section, he/she is guilty of an offence.

The circumstances in this question are similar to those in *R* v *Evans (Dorothy)* [2004] EWCA Crim 3102. In that case the appellant had been convicted of harassing her neighbours and a restraining order had been made by the court. Among other things, the order prohibited the appellant from 'using abusive words or actions' towards her neighbours. Some time into the life of the order, the neighbour called a plumber out to her house and he parked his van in the street. It was alleged that the appellant then moved her own car, which was also parked in the street, into such a position that it effectively blocked the plumber's van. The appellant was convicted of the offence of breaching the order and appealed, partly on the basis that her conduct could not properly be said to have amounted to 'abusive action'.

The Court of Appeal held that such matters should be approached in the same way as specific legislation which outlaws abusive conduct, and that a jury was entitled to conclude that, as she had been motivated by spite, the appellant's actions *could* be 'abusive' for this purpose. This was regardless of whether MURRAY's behaviour was directed at WALTON, or a third party. Answers A and D are therefore incorrect.

However, in the *Evans* case, the Court of Appeal also considered the issue of 'reasonable excuse', when it came to the defendant's understanding of the terms of the order. The court held that harassment takes many forms, and therefore the courts need to be able to prohibit conduct in fairly wide terms (e.g. in the wording of the order). It is, however, unclear just how far the defendant's subjective understanding of the terms of the order will be relevant. *If a defendant honestly believed that his/her conduct did not breach the terms of the order, this would certainly be relevant when considering whether or not he/she had a 'reasonable excuse'.* MURRAY's belief is therefore relevant, which makes answer B correct, and answer C incorrect.

General Police Duties, paras 4.6.4.13, 4.6.4.14

Answer 6.7

Answer **A** — Under s. 4(1) of the Protection from Harassment Act 1997:

> A person whose course of conduct causes another to fear, on at least two occasions, that violence will be used against him is guilty of an offence if he knows or ought to know that his course of conduct will cause the other so to fear on each of those occasions.

The course of conduct is proved because threats were made by OLTON on three occasions; however, the defendant's course of conduct must cause the victim to fear that violence *will* be used against him/her, rather than *might*. This is a strict requirement and showing that the conduct caused the victim to be seriously frightened of what might happen in the future is not enough (*R* v *Henley* [2000] Crim LR 582). Answer B is therefore incorrect.

On the other hand, s. 4 does not state that the victim must fear that *immediate* violence would be used against him/her. Answer D is therefore incorrect.

Finally, answer A is correct and answer C is incorrect, because the course of conduct for the purpose of s. 4 has to cause a person to fear, on at least two occasions, that violence would be used against *him/her*, rather than against a member of their family (*Mohammed Ali Caurti* v *DPP* [2001] EWHC Admin 867).

General Police Duties, para. 4.6.5

Answer 6.8

Answer **A** — Under section 2A(1) of the Protection from Harassment Act 1997, a person is guilty of an offence if:

- the person pursues a course of conduct in breach of s. 1(1) of the 1997 Act (i.e. a course of conduct which amounts to harassment); and
- the course of conduct amounts to stalking.

There are two matters, therefore, which need to be proved. Has the person pursued a course of conduct which amounts to harassment? Does the conduct amount to stalking? Answer C is incorrect because a course of conduct must be proved.

Section 2A(2) states that a course of conduct amounts to stalking of another person if it amounts to harassment and the person knows or ought to know that the course of conduct amounts to harassment of the other person. This section also states that the acts or omissions involved must be those that are associated with stalking; therefore, answer B is incorrect.

Section 2A(3) lists examples of behaviours associated with stalking, which include:

(a) following a person,
(b) contacting, or attempting to contact, a person by any means,
(c) publishing any statement or other material—
    (i) relating or purporting to relate to a person, or
    (ii) purporting to originate from a person,
(d) monitoring the use by a person of the internet, email or any other form of electronic communication,
(e) loitering in any place (whether public or private),
(f) interfering with any property in the possession of a person,
(g) watching or spying on a person.

Since simply monitoring a person's email amounts to an offence, answers B and D are incorrect.

General Police Duties, para. 4.6.6.1

Answer 6.9

Answer **D** — Section 4A of the Protection from Harassment Act 1997 prohibits a course of conduct relating to the offence of stalking involving fear of violence or serious alarm or distress. The first arm of the offence prohibits a course of conduct that causes the victim to fear, on at least two occasions, that violence will be used against them (which is similar to the existing s. 4 offence).

The second arm of the offence prohibits a course of conduct which causes 'serious alarm or distress' which has a 'substantial adverse effect on the day-to-day activities of the victim', which will include the victim moving home and changing the way they socialise. This is designed to recognise the serious impact that stalking may have on victims, even where an explicit fear of violence is not created by each incident of stalking behaviour. Answers A and B are incorrect as the offence may be committed when *either* of these outcomes is present and BERRY has most certainly changed her lifestyle as a result of TROTT's behaviour.

The issue of a 'course of conduct' relating to the s. 4 offence was addressed in *R (On the Application of A)* v *DPP* [2004] EWHC 2454 (Admin). In this case, the defendant's conduct on the first occasion (e.g. a threat to burn the victim's house down) did not cause the victim undue concern, but a second threat some time later to do the same thing *did* put the victim in fear of violence, partly because this was the second time the threat had been made. The defendant argued that the victim had only been put in fear of violence by his threats to burn her house down on the second occasion, and therefore there had been no course of conduct (i.e. the victim had only feared violence on one occasion, as opposed to the two occasions that were required by the section). The Divisional Court disagreed and held that the magistrates were entitled to find as a matter of fact that the two incidents had put the victim in fear of violence, notwithstanding her admission that, on the first occasion, she had not been too concerned. While this case relates to a different offence, the elements for a course of conduct will be the same for s. 4 and s. 4A, and therefore answer C is incorrect.

General Police Duties, paras 4.6.5, 4.6.6.2

Answer 6.10

Answer **C** — Section 42 of the Criminal Justice and Police Act 2001 provides a discretionary power to give directions to people in the vicinity. The power arises where:

- the person is outside (or in the vicinity of) any premises that are used by any individual as his/her dwelling; and
- the constable believes, on reasonable grounds, that the person is there for the purpose of representing or persuading the resident (or anyone else)
  - that he/she should not do something he/she is entitled or required to do; or
  - that he/she should do something that he/she is under no obligation to do; and
- the constable also believes, on reasonable grounds, that the person's presence amounts to, or is likely to result in, the harassment of the resident or is likely to cause alarm or distress to the resident.

The discretionary power is available to the most senior ranking police officer at the scene (PS PURCELL), making answers A, B and D incorrect.

General Police Duties, para. 4.6.6

Answer 6.11

Answer **C** — There is no requirement that the officer giving a direction using the power under s. 42 of the Criminal Justice and Police Act 2001 be in uniform (making answer B incorrect), nor is there any requirement that the direction be given in writing (it can be given orally), making answer D incorrect. Answer A is incorrect as the power is available when the person to whom the direction is going to be given is outside (or in the vicinity of) any premises that are used by any individual as his/her dwelling (correct answer C). Even if the protesters were acting in a way that caused workers at the financial institution harassment, alarm or distress, the power would still not be available.

General Police Duties, para. 4.6.7

Answer 6.12

Answer **B** — Section 29C of the Public Order Act 1986 deals with the publication and distribution of written material which is threatening and the person publishing or distributing the material *intends* thereby to stir up religious hatred. Unlike the similar offence under s. 19 of the Act (publishing or distributing material in respect of *racial* hatred), this offence does not contain the proviso which states that having regard to all the circumstances the publication or distribution of the material is likely to stir up such hatred. Therefore, the only way this can be committed is with that intention to stir up religious hatred. This means PERRY does not commit the offence and so answers A and C are incorrect. Clearly the offence is committed by BRYANT (the publisher), meaning that answer D is incorrect.

General Police Duties, para. 4.6.2.6

7 | Anti-social Behaviour

STUDY PREPARATION

The Anti-social Behaviour, Crime and Policing Act 2014 completely overhauled the previous ASBO system and simplifies powers to deal with anti-social behaviour.

These measures feature highly in regional and local policing strategies to tackle crime and the fear of crime. This makes them important, not only to police officers but also, as a result, to those training and examining police law.

QUESTIONS

Question 7.1

The police and local authority are holding a strategy meeting to discuss McCANN, who is 10 years of age. Numerous referrals have been made to the anti-social behaviour coordinator over several months, showing evidence that McCANN has been acting in an anti-social manner towards PATEL, an elderly next-door neighbour who lives alone.

Given that McCANN has acted in an anti-social manner against PATEL, could a civil injunction under Part 1 of the Anti-social Behaviour, Crime and Policing Act 2014 be applied for in these circumstances?

A Yes, provided McCANN's conduct amounts to anti-social behaviour, an injunction may be granted.

B No, even if the conduct amounts to anti-social behaviour, an injunction cannot be granted because of McCANN's age.

C Yes, if the conduct amounts to anti-social behaviour an injunction may be granted; McCANN's age is not relevant in an application for a civil injunction.

D No, because only one person in another household has been affected by McCANN's behaviour.

Question 7.2

The court has granted a civil injunction against KANE, aged 19, for conduct which amounted to anti-social behaviour. The court has decided that because drug misuse had been a major cause of the behaviour that led to the injunction being made, it would be appropriate for KANE to comply with a drug rehabilitation programme.

What is the maximum period of time the court can specify for KANE to comply with the injunction?

A A maximum period of six months.
B A minimum period of twelve months.
C A maximum period of two years.
D There is no maximum period.

Question 7.3

PENGELLI is 13 years of age and is appearing before the court for failing to comply with a civil injunction. An injunction was previously issued requiring PENGELLI not to drink alcohol in public places; however, the court has heard that she has continued a pattern of behaviour which involves her regularly drinking in public places and behaving in an anti-social manner. An application is now being made for a supervision order against PENGELLI and the prosecutor is considering applying for her to be placed on a curfew, with an electronic monitoring requirement to be attached to it.

Would an application by the prosecutor for these restrictions be likely to succeed?

A No, PENGELLI is under 14 and cannot be made subject to a curfew as part of the supervision order.
B Yes, PENGELLI can be made subject to a curfew, with an electronic monitoring requirement to be attached to it in these circumstances.
C No, PENGELLI may be made subject to a curfew as part of the supervision order, but the court cannot make an electronic monitoring requirement part of the order.
D No, PENGELLI is under 16 and cannot be made subject to a curfew or an electronic monitoring requirement as part of the order.

Question 7.4

MURRAY, aged 21, was convicted by the magistrates' court for an offence contrary to s. 5 of the Public Order Act 1986, following abusive behaviour towards an elderly neighbour, and was given a conditional discharge for the offence. Prior to sentence, the court heard that MURRAY was alcohol-dependent and was regularly involved in abusing people in the street when drunk. Several intervention initiatives had been attempted, but had failed because of MURRAY's continuous drinking.

In these circumstances, would it be suitable for the prosecutor to ask the court to make a Criminal Behaviour Order in relation to MURRAY?

A No, MURRAY has only been given a conditional discharge for the offence.
B Yes, provided the police and local authority have consulted before the case and that one of these partners supports the application.
C Yes, provided either the police or the local authority supports the application.
D Yes, a prosecutor can make such a request regardless of the wishes of the police or local authority.

Question 7.5

The court has granted a Criminal Behaviour Order against SHAW, aged 16, for conduct which amounted to anti-social behaviour. The court has decided that because drunkenness had been a significant contributing factor to the behaviour that led to the Criminal Behaviour Order being made, it would be appropriate for the order to require SHAW not to consume alcohol in a public place.

Which of the following statements is correct in relation to the time period the court can specify for SHAW to comply with the order?

A The order should be set for a minimum period of six months.
B The order should be set for a minimum period of one year.
C The order should be set for a minimum period of two years.
D There is no minimum period for the order to be set.

Question 7.6

Constable DONAHUE is the community beat officer on a housing estate, which has been suffering an ongoing youth annoyance problem outside a small shopping centre. One bank holiday weekend, the police were called to the location to deal with intimidation and annoyance towards shopkeepers and customers, on average 20 times a day.

Constable DONAHUE was on duty on the bank holiday Monday and visited the shopping centre during the afternoon. There were two youths present who the officer knew were the main instigators. After speaking to the shopkeepers, Constable DONAHUE formed the opinion that there would be further harassment that afternoon and evening. Constable DONAHUE was considering whether an order should be given under s. 34(1) of the Anti-social Behaviour, Crime and Policing Act 2014, to disperse the two youths before the problem escalated again.

Would an order under s. 34(1) be appropriate in these circumstances?

A   No, because there are only two people present.

B   Yes, because there are two or more people present.

C   No, this power may not be used at such short notice.

D   Yes, a direction may be necessary to prevent anti-social behaviour regardless of how many people are present.

Question 7.7

Constable DEAN was on patrol at 7.30 pm in a housing estate where, following incidents of significant and persistent anti-social behaviour, a dispersal notice had been issued. Constable DEAN saw PURSE, aged 15, and CHALMERS, aged 16, staggering around shouting loudly and clearly drunk. Constable DEAN was concerned that they would continue to act in an anti-social manner if left at the location.

Would Constable DEAN have the power to take PURSE and CHALMERS home in these circumstances, utilising powers under s. 3 of the Anti-social Behaviour, Crime and Policing Act 2014 (power to remove people to their place of residence)?

A   No, this power would only be available in relation to PURSE.

B   No, these powers only apply between the hours of 9 pm and 6 am.

C   Yes, as they are likely to commit anti-social behaviour.

D   Yes, provided they have been instructed to leave the area and have refused.

Question 7.8

PCSO McLEAN works on a Neighbourhood Policing Team and has been consulting with the local authority about a shop on a housing estate which has been the subject of numerous complaints in recent neighbourhood meetings. The shop is open late every night and young people congregate outside depositing litter in the street. PCSO McLEAN has spoken to the shop owner several times, who has stated that the local authority is tasked with clearing up litter, not business owners. Consideration is being given to issuing the owner with a Community Protection Notice under Part 5 of the Anti-social, Crime and Policing Act 2014.

Which of the following statements is correct in relation to the issuing of such a notice?

A The notice may only be issued by the local authority as this is an environmental issue.

B The notice may be issued by the local authority or any police constable.

C The notice may be issued by the local authority or any police constable, provided it has been authorised by an inspector.

D The notice may be issued by the local authority or the police, including designated PCSOs.

Question 7.9

A house in a neighbourhood has been the source of numerous complaints by residents because of weekend all-night parties and the significant disorder they attract. The premises are owned by RAWLINGS, who rents them out to a tenant, who only uses them on weekends to hold the parties. The police have been unsuccessful in trying to speak to RAWLINGS or the tenant and they have decided to issue a closure notice. Inspector MEDINA wishes to enter the premises and post notices before the next party and has been in discussion with the manager of the local authority housing department about the best way to secure the premises after the notice has been posted.

Who is authorised to enter the premises to secure them in these circumstances—the police or the local authority?

A Only the police, because the premises are privately owned.

B Either organisation, provided they have consulted with each other about the notice.

C Only the police, because the notice is being issued by them.

D Either organisation, but if force is to be used, a member of the local authority must be accompanied by a police officer.

Question 7.10

Constable ELSOM is part of a Neighbourhood Policing Team and has been liaising with the local authority about premises that have been subject to a number of complaints at public meetings because of persistent anti-social behaviour problems.

A closure notice has been issued in respect of the premises and an application is being prepared for a closure order to be issued by the court.

When must the application for a closure order be taken before the court?

A The application must be heard by the court not later than 24 hours after service of the closure notice.

B The application must be heard by the court not later than 48 hours after service of the closure notice.

C The application must be heard by the court not later than one week after service of the closure notice.

D The application must be heard by the court not later than one month after service of the closure notice.

Question 7.11

Reliable intelligence is received that a large gathering of youths is planned to take place on a housing estate. The intelligence states that a number of high-powered vehicles will be used to race around the housing estate and that this racing will be watched and encouraged by over 100 youths. This intelligence is passed to Inspector EMERY who is considering using the powers under Part 3 of the Anti-social Behaviour, Crime and Policing Act 2014 to authorise a dispersal order (under s. 34 of the Act) to counter and reduce the likelihood of anti-social behaviour occurring.

Could Inspector EMERY authorise the dispersal power in this situation?

A Yes, although any authorisation would be limited to a maximum period of 48 hours.

B No, as the power can only be authorised by an officer of the rank of superintendent or above.

C Yes, although the power to direct people to leave the specified area can only be used when the person concerned has committed an act of anti-social behaviour.

D No, as the power under s. 34 can only be authorised when anti-social behaviour has actually taken place.

Question 7.12

An authorisation under s. 34 of the Anti-social Behaviour, Crime and Policing Act 2014 has been granted in respect of a shopping precinct. The intelligence that gave rise to the authorisation being granted included information that youths would be causing criminal damage to buildings using cans of spray paint. During the time period that authorisation under s. 34 is valid, PC NIELD (on uniform foot patrol in the shopping precinct) lawfully stops and searches AYLING (who is 15 years old) using the power of stop and search under s. 1 of the Police and Criminal Evidence Act 1984. During the course of the search, the officer finds a can of spray paint in a bag that AYLING is carrying. PC NIELD directs AYLING to leave the shopping precinct and not to return for 24 hours.

Would PC NIELD be able to seize the can of spray paint from AYLING using powers under the Anti-social, Crime and Policing Act 2014?

A No, as an authorisation under s. 34 provides a power to disperse individuals or groups from an area—it does not provide a power to seize items.

B Yes, the can of spray paint can be seized and retained indefinitely.

C No, the power of seizure associated with the authorisation relates to the seizure of alcohol alone.

D Yes, but it must not be returned to AYLING before the exclusion period (in this case 24 hours) is over.

ANSWERS

Answer 7.1

Answer **A** — Part 1 of the Anti-social Behaviour, Crime and Policing Act 2014 creates the power for a civil court to grant injunctions if it is satisfied, on the balance of probabilities, that the respondent has engaged or threatened to engage in anti-social behaviour and it is just and convenient to grant the injunction for the purpose of preventing the respondent from engaging in anti-social behaviour.

Section 2(1) of the 2014 Act defines 'anti-social behaviour' as:

(a) conduct that has caused, or is likely to cause, harassment, alarm or distress to any person, or
(b) conduct capable of causing nuisance or annoyance to a person in relation to that person's occupation of residential premises, or
(c) conduct capable of causing housing-related nuisance or annoyance to any person.

The 2014 Act requires the person to have engaged in conduct that has caused, or is likely to cause, harassment, alarm or distress to *any person* regardless of where they live. Answer D is therefore incorrect.

A court may only grant an injunction against a person aged 10 or over (s. 1(1)); therefore, answers B and C are incorrect.

General Police Duties, para. 4.7.2, 4.7.2.2

Answer 7.2

Answer **D** — Part 1 of the Anti-social Behaviour, Crime and Policing Act 2014 creates the power for a civil court to grant injunctions if it is satisfied, on the balance of probabilities, that the respondent has engaged or threatened to engage in anti-social behaviour and it is just and convenient to grant the injunction for the purpose of preventing the respondent from engaging in anti-social behaviour.

The court may attach conditions to the injunction (such as attending a drug rehabilitation programme) and specify the person (an individual or an organisation) who is responsible for supervising compliance.

There is no minimum or maximum term for the injunction for adults, so the court may decide that the injunction should be for a specified period or an indefinite period (however, in the case of injunctions against under-18s, the maximum term is 12 months).

Answers A, B and C are therefore incorrect.

General Police Duties, para. 4.7.2.4

Answer 7.3

Answer **B** — A breach of an injunction by someone aged under 18 could result in the youth court imposing a supervision order or a detention order; however, a detention order can only be imposed when the court considers that the severity or extent of the behaviour warrants it and that no other sanction available to it is appropriate. In this case, an application for a supervision order is appropriate and the court must be satisfied beyond reasonable doubt that the under-18 has, without reasonable excuse, breached the injunction.

There are certain restrictions in respect of a young person's age; for example, a detention order cannot be imposed on a person under the age of 14. However, there are no such restrictions in relation to a supervision order, which may be made against any person appearing before the court (provided they are over the age of 10).

A supervision order may contain one or more of the following requirements: a supervision requirement, an activity requirement or a curfew requirement. An electronic monitoring requirement may be attached to a curfew requirement in order to monitor compliance. Since this applies to all persons over the age of 10, answers A, C and D are incorrect.

General Police Duties, para. 4.7.2.7

Answer 7.4

Answer **C** — Part 2 of the Anti-social Behaviour, Crime and Policing Act 2014 creates the Criminal Behaviour Order (CBO). An order may only be made against an offender when he/she has been sentenced for the offence or given a conditional discharge (s. 22(6)) (however, no order may be made where the offender has been given an absolute discharge or has only been bound over to keep the peace). Answer A is therefore incorrect.

The legislation has deliberately kept formal consultation requirements to a minimum, to enable agencies to act quickly where needed to protect victims and communities. The previous requirement (under the Crime and Disorder Act 1998) for the police and local authority to consult before the application is made no longer exists (unless the offender is under 18, when the prosecution must find out the views of the local youth offending team before applying for the CBO). Although it is accepted that in most cases the statutory partners will probably have consulted as part of their strategies for dealing with anti-social behaviour, under the 2014 Act either of the statutory partners may make the request of their own volition and answer B is incorrect.

On the other hand, a court will only be able to make a CBO against an offender if the prosecutor applies for it following advice from either the police or the local authority. Answer D is therefore incorrect.

General Police Duties, para. 4.7.3.1

Answer 7.5

Answer **B** — Part 2 of the Anti-social Behaviour, Crime and Policing Act 2014 creates the Criminal Behaviour Order (CBO). Unlike civil injunctions (granted under Part 1), there are set periods and the terms of the CBO must include the duration of the order. For adults, there is a minimum of two years up to an indefinite period.

For orders given to people under the age of 18, there is a minimum period of 12 months and a maximum period of three years.

Answers A, C and D are therefore incorrect.

General Police Duties, para. 4.7.3.5

Answer 7.6

Answer **D** — Part 3 of the Anti-social Behaviour, Crime and Policing Act 2014 established a dispersal power that enables officers (constables in uniform and PCSOs) to direct a person who has committed, or is likely to commit, anti-social behaviour to leave a specified area and not return for a specified period of up to 48 hours.

The dispersal power can only be used where an officer of at least the rank of inspector has authorised its use in a specified locality (s. 34(1)) and the inspector reasonably believes that the exercise of the dispersal powers may be required in order to remove or reduce the likelihood of the anti-social behaviour occurring. There is no requirement to consult with the local authority or publicise the dispersal notice in advance; the notice under the 2014 Act may be used spontaneously, provided the appropriate authorisation is given in writing. Answer C is therefore incorrect.

Again, unlike the 2003 Act, there is no requirement for at least two people to be present before the power may be used to disperse people. A direction may be given to 'a person' to leave the area and not return.

Answers A and B are therefore incorrect.

General Police Duties, para. 4.7.4

Answer 7.7

Answer **A** — Part 3 of the Anti-social Behaviour, Crime and Policing Act 2014 contains a dispersal power that enables officers (constables in uniform and PCSOs) to direct a person who has committed, or is likely to commit, anti-social behaviour to leave a specified area and not return for a specified period of up to 48 hours.

The dispersal power can only be used where an officer of at least the rank of inspector has authorised its use in a specified locality (s. 34(1)) and the inspector reasonably believes that the exercise of the dispersal powers may be required in order to remove or reduce the likelihood of the anti-social behaviour occurring.

The officer must specify the area from which the person is excluded, and may specify when and by which route they must leave the area (s. 35(5)(b) and (c)). Where the officer believes that an individual is under the age of 16, an officer can remove that individual to a place where he/she lives or to a place of safety (s. 35(7)). There is no requirement to have warned an individual before utilising the power to take them home and since this power only applies to those under the age of 16, answers C and D are incorrect.

No time restrictions apply under the 2014 Act, so answer B is incorrect.

General Police Duties, para. 4.7.4.2

Answer 7.8

Answer **D** — Part 4 of the Anti-social, Crime and Policing Act 2014 deals with Community Protection Notices (CPNs). The notice is intended to deal with unreasonable, ongoing problems or nuisances which negatively affect the community's quality of life by targeting the person responsible (s. 43(1)). The notice can direct any individual over the age of 16, business or organisation responsible to stop causing the problem and it could also require the person responsible to take reasonable steps to ensure that it does not occur again (s. 43(3)).

Generally, local authorities are likely to take the lead in dealing with these kinds of issues and they will continue to be able to issue the new notice. However, the power to issue a notice will also be available to the police and PCSOs, if designated by the chief constable (s. 53(5)). Answers A and B are incorrect.

There is no requirement for an officer of the rank of inspector to authorise notices under this section; therefore, answer C is incorrect.

General Police Duties, paras 4.7.5, 4.7.5.1

Answer 7.9

Answer **B** — A closure notice may be issued either by the police or the local authority, under s. 76 of the Anti-social Behaviour, Crime and Policing Act 2014. Before issuing the notice, the police or local authority must consult any person or agency they consider appropriate, and must also make reasonable efforts to inform the owner, landlord, licensee and anyone who appears to be residing in the premises (s. 76(6) and (7)).

Section 79(4) provides an authorised person with a power of entry to the premises, using reasonable force if necessary, to secure the notice to the premises. The authorised person may be a police officer or a member of the local authority, regardless of the organisation issuing the notice; answer C is therefore incorrect.

There is no requirement under s. 76 for a member of either organisation to be accompanied by the other to enter premises by force—they are only required to consult with the appropriate person or agency. Answer D is incorrect.

The fact that the premises are privately owned will not bar the local authority from becoming involved, therefore, answer A is incorrect.

General Police Duties, para. 4.7.5.2

Answer 7.10

Answer **B** — When a closure notice is issued, the police or local authority must apply to the magistrates' court for a closure order (s. 80(1)). The magistrates' court must hear the application for the closure order within 48 hours of the closure notice being issued (excluding Christmas Day) unless the closure notice has been cancelled by a cancellation notice (s. 80(3)).

Answers A, C and D are therefore incorrect.

General Police Duties, para. 4.7.5.3

Answer 7.11

Answer **A** — Answer B is incorrect as the dispersal power can be authorised by an officer of the rank of inspector or above (s. 34(1)). Answer D is incorrect as the authorisation can only be given where the police officer of or above the rank of inspector reasonably believes that, in respect of any locality within their police area, the exercise of the dispersal powers in Part 3 of the Act may be required in order to remove or reduce the likelihood of the anti-social behaviour occurring. For instance, the inspector may have intelligence to indicate that there is likely to be anti-social behaviour on a particular housing estate during the weekend and authorise the use of the dispersal for 48 hours—this is a power to prevent as well as deal with ongoing anti-social behaviour. Answer C is incorrect as Part 3 of the Anti-social Behaviour, Crime and Policing Act 2014 provides a dispersal power that enables officers (constables in uniform and police community support officers (PCSOs)) to direct a person who has committed, or is likely to commit, anti-social behaviour to leave a specified area and not return for a specified period of up to 48 hours—so it is not limited to those who have actually carried out anti-social behaviour.

General Police Duties, paras 4.7.4, 4.7.4.1

Answer 7.12

Answer **D** — An officer would be able to require an individual to hand over items causing, or likely to cause, anti-social behaviour—for instance, alcohol or a can of spray paint (s. 37), meaning that answers A and C are incorrect. Answer B is incorrect as the officer does not have power under this provision to retain any seized item indefinitely. The officer must give the person information in writing about how and when they can recover the item, which must not be returned before the exclusion period is over (in the circumstances of the question, that exclusion period is 24 hours), meaning that answer D is correct.

General Police Duties, para. 4.7.4.2

8 | Offences Involving Communications

QUESTIONS

Question 8.1

Until recently, MELLOR worked for a company that owned five nightclubs. MELLOR was the manager of one of the clubs, but was sacked after falling out with the owner, BOYD. On a busy Saturday night, between midnight and 12.30 am, MELLOR rang the receptionist at each of the five clubs stating that there was a bomb at one of the premises. MELLOR then texted BOYD with the same message. MELLOR was deliberately unspecific about the location, intending to cause maximum disruption, hoping that each premises would be evacuated.

Which of the following statements is correct in relation to MELLOR's liability under s. 51(2) of the Criminal Law Act 1977 (bomb hoaxes)?

A Provided the intention was to cause the receptionist at each premises to fear that a bomb was likely to explode, MELLOR could be guilty of this offence.
B Provided the intention was to cause any person to fear that a bomb was likely to explode, MELLOR could be guilty of this offence.
C Provided the intention was to cause BOYD to fear that a bomb was likely to explode, MELLOR could be guilty of this offence.
D This section requires the offender to be specific about the location of the alleged threat; MELLOR could not be guilty of this offence as the message was too vague.

Question 8.2

Leading up to Christmas, HULL had ordered a number of items on Amazon and eBay and was expecting the packages to be delivered by post. HULL received one parcel addressed to a neighbour, WILLIS, which was delivered by mistake. HULL opened the package.

Section 84(3) of the Postal Services Act 2000 outlines an offence committed by a person who opens a postal package that was incorrectly delivered to him/her. What must be shown in relation to HULL's state of mind, if this offence were to be proved?

A That HULL acted to the neighbour's detriment and knew, or reasonably suspected, that the package had been incorrectly delivered.
B That intending to act to another person's detriment and without reasonable excuse, HULL opened the package knowing, or reasonably suspecting, that the package had been incorrectly delivered.
C That intending to make a gain and without reasonable excuse, HULL opened the package knowing that the package had been incorrectly delivered.
D That HULL knew, or reasonably suspected, that by opening the package it would be delayed in arriving with the neighbour.

Question 8.3

ANDREWS runs a general store on a housing estate. The shop contains a counter within the premises that acts as an agent for the Post Office, providing a general postal service. LIMOUTH is a local resident whom ANDREWS had previously banned from the premises for shoplifting. LIMOUTH entered the store one day to use the post office counter to pay a bill. ANDREWS threatened to call the police if LIMOUTH did not leave immediately.

Which of the following statements is correct in relation to the power to remove a person from premises, under s. 88(4) of the Postal Services Act 2000?

A ANDREWS has the power to remove LIMOUTH under s. 88(4) at this point, before the arrival of the police.

B Section 88(4) does not create a power for members of the public to remove people from premises however, the police may do so when they arrive.

C ANDREWS does not have the power to remove LIMOUTH under s. 88(4), because these premises are not covered by the Postal Services Act 2000.

D ANDREWS does not have the power to remove him under s. 88(4), without any further adverse behaviour by LIMOUTH.

Question 8.4

BOLIN was expecting delivery of an important parcel. He had to leave his house for a short time and on return he drove into the street as a van belonging to a national parcel delivery service was being driven away. BOLIN followed the van to the next delivery address and approached the driver, QUINLAN, asking whether she had a parcel for him. QUINLAN stated that parcels could only be delivered to an address and that if BOLIN's parcel was on the van, it would be delivered the next day. BOLIN became angry and blocked in QUINLAN's van, refusing to move until she handed over his parcel. QUINLAN called the police and Constable NORTON arrived a short while later.

Considering offences and powers under s. 88 of the Postal Services Act 2000, which of the following statements is correct?

A Constable NORTON is required under this section to remove BOLIN from the scene, or assist QUINLAN to do so.

B Constable NORTON is required under this section to remove BOLIN, or assist QUINLAN; however, QUINLAN had the power to do so herself.

C BOLIN has committed an offence under this section by obstructing QUINLAN; however, the power to remove people only applies in a post office or related premises.

D BOLIN has committed no offence under this section; the offence only relates to an obstruction caused in a post office or related premises.

Question 8.5

BURTON was undergoing an acrimonious separation from his partner, HASTINGS, who had started seeing another person, GRANT. BURTON managed to find out where GRANT was working and left a message with a colleague. BURTON asked the person answering the phone to pass an urgent message to GRANT, stating that HASTINGS was in hospital after a car crash and had suffered life-threatening injuries. The story was completely false.

Considering the offence under s. 1 of the Malicious Communications Act 1988, which of the following statements is correct?

A This was not a threatening or indecent message; therefore, this offence is incomplete.

B The offence would only be complete if it was BURTON's intention to cause GRANT anxiety or distress.

C The offence would be complete if it was BURTON's intention to cause GRANT or any other person anxiety or distress.

D The offence would only be complete if BURTON intended causing anxiety or distress to the person he actually spoke to, which in these circumstances was unlikely.

Question 8.6

POOLE owns a property which he is renting out privately to REECE. REECE has failed to pay the rent for the last three months and despite calling at the premises several times in the last month, POOLE has been unable to collect the money owed to him. In desperation, POOLE sent a text message to REECE which said, 'I'm coming to reclaim my property Monday and if you are there, I'm going to personally throw you into the street'. REECE was fearful because of the contents of the text and contacted the police.

Section 1(2) of the Malicious Communications Act 1988 outlines a defence for someone who sends a message which amounts to a threat. In respect of this defence, what would POOLE have to show in order to avoid prosecution for this offence?

A POOLE would have to show that he did not intend the message to be threatening.

B POOLE would have to show that an ordinary person would think the demands were reasonable.

C POOLE would have to show that he reasonably believed that the threat was a proper means of enforcing the demand.

D POOLE would have to show that there were reasonable grounds for making the demand, that he believed the threat was a proper means of enforcing the demand and that reasonable grounds existed for that belief.

Question 8.7

HEALD was infatuated with his neighbour, FARR, and continually asked her out on dates. FARR was flattered and not at all threatened by this, but refused to go out with him. HEALD then made an indecent phone call to FARR in an effort to 'turn her on'. HEALD did not, however, intend FARR to be distressed by these calls. She was not threatened and found it all mildly amusing.

Does HEALD commit the offence outlined in s. 127 of the Communications Act 2003 of improper use of a public electronic communications network?

A Yes, but only if it can be proved the phone call was grossly offensive.

B Yes, even though HEALD did not intend to cause distress and FARR was not distressed by the call.

C No, HEALD did not make persistent use of a public electronic communications network.

D No, FARR was not caused annoyance, inconvenience or needless anxiety by the call.

Question 8.8

GOODHEW is vehemently opposed to certain activities of the United States of America which are associated with the foreign policy of that country. GOODHEW sends a letter from his home city of Newcastle to the United States Embassy in Nine Elms, London and also sends a letter to the President of the United States in Washington (United States of America). Both letters state that they contain the poison Ricin. GOODHEW has sprinkled a small amount of flour inside each letter intending that this will make any person receiving the letters believe they contain a noxious substance that will endanger life and this will consequently cause panic and disruption.

Has GOODHEW committed an offence under s. 114 of the Anti-terrorism, Crime and Security Act 2001?

A Yes, the offence has been committed in respect of both letters.

B No, because GOODHEW did not intend to induce a belief in some other person that the letters contained an explosive substance or one that was likely to ignite.

C Yes, but only in respect of the letter sent to the United States Embassy in London.

D No, because GOODHEW did not intend to cause personal injury or damage to property as a result of the letters being sent.

Question 8.9

COKER (who lives in Exeter) and WINGFIELD (who lives in Preston) meet by way of an Internet chat room. They communicate regularly and discuss the fact that they both have unusual sexual fetishes including the desire to have sexual intercourse with animals. A week after discussing their sexual desires, COKER contacts WINGFIELD stating that he has actually had sexual intercourse with a dog and asks if WINGFIELD would like to see pictures of the sexual activity. WINGFIELD states that he would and asks for the pictures to be posted to him and sends COKER his home address in Preston. COKER sends the pictures to WINGFIELD, but accidentally addresses it to house number 11 rather than 111 and consequently the pictures arrive at a house owned by HIRD (rather than WINGFIELD), who opens the envelope and is distressed and offended at the content, which he feels is obscene.

Considering only the offence under s. 85 of the Postal Services Act 2000 (sending prohibited articles by post), has COKER committed an offence?

A No, as the articles sent are pictures rather than articles which are made, intended or adapted to cause injury to another person.

B Yes, and the state of mind of the recipient (HIRD) is essential in proving the offence as the recipient must be caused alarm or distress by the content of the article.

C No, as it was not COKER's intention to cause offence to HIRD.

D Yes, and whether HIRD finds the content of the article obscene or not is irrelevant as whether an article is obscene or not is a question of fact for the court to determine in each case.

Question 8.10

WALDER holds a grudge against the Post Office and has made a number of complaints about what he describes as substandard service in delivering mail to the small village where he resides. He wants to get support for his complaints from other village residents and decides to sabotage the mail being delivered to his village. He visits the Post Office depot that delivers mail to his village and manages to get inside the depot and into the sorting rooms. He sees several bags of post which he believes are destined to be sent to residents of the village and, intending to delay the course of their transmission, he takes them into a storage cupboard to hide them. Once inside the cupboard, his curiosity gets the better of him and he opens one of the mail-bags to see what it contains. He finds several letters addressed to other residents of the village and decides to open them to look at the contents. One of the letters is addressed to his neighbour and contains an offer of employment with the Post Office. Outraged, WALDER destroys the letter.

At what point does WALDER commit the offence of misuse and obstruction of the postal services (contrary to s. 84(1) of the Postal Services Act 2000)?

A When he hides the mail-bags in the storage cupboard.

B When he opens the mail-bag.

C When he opens the letter addressed to his neighbour.

D When he destroys the letter.

ANSWERS

Answer 8.1

Answer **B** — Under s. 51(2) of the Criminal Law Act 1977, a person who communicates any information which he/she knows or believes to be false to another person with the intention of inducing in him/her or any other person a false belief that a bomb or other thing liable to explode or ignite is present in any place or location whatever is guilty of an offence.

There is no need for the person making the communication to have any particular person in mind at the time the threat is made (s. 51(3)); therefore, answers A and C are incorrect.

It has been held that while the information communicated need not be specific, a message saying that there is a bomb somewhere has been held to be enough, even though no location was given (*R* v *Webb* (1995) 92(27) LSG 31). Answer D is therefore incorrect.

General Police Duties, para. 4.8.3

Answer 8.2

Answer **B** — Under s. 84(3) of the Postal Services Act 2000, a person commits an offence if, intending to act to a person's detriment and without reasonable excuse, he/she opens a postal packet which he/she knows or reasonably suspects has been incorrectly delivered to him/her.

The 'intent' element of this offence is important; it must be shown that the person:

- opened the package;
- knowing or reasonably suspecting that it had been incorrectly delivered to him/her; and that
- he/she did so intending 'to act to another person's detriment' (this can be any other person's detriment, not simply the addressee's).

Answer B contains the only correct combination; therefore, answers A, C and D are incorrect.

(Note that there is a separate offence under s. 84(1) of delaying a package, but this offence would not apply in these circumstances because the person must be shown to have intentionally delayed or opened a postal packet in the course of its transmission by post.)

General Police Duties, para. 4.8.4

Answer 8.3

Answer **D** — Under s. 88(1) of the Postal Services Act 2000, a person commits an offence if, without reasonable excuse, he/she obstructs a person engaged in the business in connection with the provision of a universal postal service, or obstructs the course of business of any universal postal service post office or related premises.

Under s. 88(3), a person commits a further offence if without reasonable excuse, he/she fails to leave a universal postal service post office or related premises when required to do so by a person who is engaged in the business of a universal service provider, and reasonably suspects him of committing an offence under subs. (1).

Section 88(4) provides that a person who commits an offence under subs. (3) may be removed by any person engaged in the business of a universal service provider.

This needs to be viewed as a step-by-step process; a person may be removed from premises using the power under s. 88(3) when he/she has first committed an offence under s. 88(1) *and* then refused to leave the relevant premises having committed an offence under s. 88(3). Returning to the scenario in this question, LIMOUTH has neither caused an obstruction nor has he failed to leave at this stage. Therefore, without any further adverse behaviour by him, there is no power to remove him from the premises at this stage. Answer A is therefore incorrect.

Anyone failing to leave when properly required to do so under subs. (3) may be removed by the post office staff but also, subs. (5) provides that '*any constable shall on demand remove, or assist in removing, any such person*'. Whilst this places a clear duty on individual police officers to help in removing offenders under these circumstances, post office staff may do so independently of the police and answer B is therefore incorrect.

Finally, 'related premises' are any premises belonging to a universal postal service post office *or* used together with any such post office (s. 88(6)), which would cover the type of premises in this scenario. Answer C is therefore incorrect.

General Police Duties, para. 4.8.4.2

Answer 8.4

Answer **C** — Under s. 88(1) of the Postal Services Act 2000, a person commits an offence if he/she obstructs a person engaged in the business of a universal service provider in the execution of his/her duty in connection with the provision of a universal postal service, *or* obstructs, while in any universal postal service post office or related premises, the course of business of a universal service provider. Since the obstruction offence may be committed in either of these circumstances, answer D is incorrect.

Under s. 88(5), a constable *shall* on demand remove, or assist in removing, any person who has committed an obstruction under this section and has without reasonable excuse failed to leave when required to do so by someone engaged in the postal provider's business. However, the power to remove a person only applies when he/she has committed an obstruction in a post office or related premises, and has refused to leave there. Answer A is therefore incorrect (although, of course, there may be offences committed under other Acts of Parliament).

Finally, under s. 88(4), a person who commits an offence under subs. (3) *may* be removed by any person engaged in the business of a universal service provider. Again, this power only relates to an offence committed on post office or related premises, and therefore answer B is incorrect.

General Police Duties, para. 4.8.4.2

Answer 8.5

Answer **C** — Under s. 1(1)(a) of the Malicious Communications Act 1988, a person commits an offence if he or she sends to another person a letter, electronic communication or article of any description which conveys:

(i) a message which is indecent or grossly offensive;
(ii) a threat; or
(iii) information which is false and known or believed to be false by the sender; …

The offence is not restricted to threatening or indecent communications and can include giving false information and answer A is incorrect.

It must be shown that one of the sender's purposes in so doing is to cause distress or anxiety, which may be intended towards the recipient or *any other person*. Answer B is therefore incorrect.

The offence can be committed by using someone else unconnected to the situation to send, deliver or transmit a message. It is not necessary to show that the defendant intended to cause *that* person anxiety or distress and answer D is incorrect.

General Police Duties, para. 4.8.5

Answer 8.6

Answer **D** — The wording of the statutory defence has been changed (by the Criminal Justice and Police Act 2001) to make the relevant test objective. It will no longer be enough that the person claiming the defence under s. 1(2) believed that he/she had reasonable grounds; the defendant will have to show that:

- there were in fact reasonable grounds for making the demand;
- he/she believed that the accompanying threat was a proper means of enforcing the demand; and
- reasonable grounds existed for that belief.

Answer D contains the only correct combination; therefore, answers A, B and C are incorrect.

General Police Duties, para. 4.8.5.1

Answer 8.7

Answer **B** — Section 127 of the Communications Act 2003 contains two separate offences. Under s. 127(1), a person is guilty of an offence if he/she:

(a) sends by means of a public electronic communications network a message or other matter that is grossly offensive or of an indecent, obscene or menacing character; or

(b) causes any such message or matter to be so sent.

Since the offence may be committed by sending a message that is grossly offensive *or* of an indecent character, answer A is incorrect.

The offence under subs. (1) is designed to deal with nuisance calls, and the offence is complete when the defendant sends the relevant message or other matter that is, as a matter of fact, indecent, obscene or menacing. There is no need to show intention on the part of the defendant, nor any resultant distress caused (answer D is therefore incorrect). The offence is complete by simply making an indecent phone call.

The separate offence under s. 127(2) of the Act *does* deal with causing annoyance, inconvenience or needless anxiety to another. Under this section, a person is guilty of an offence when they send or cause a message by means of a public electronic communications network that he/she knows to be false, or persistently makes use of such a network. However, since the behaviour of the person in this scenario is covered by s. 127(1), the offence is complete and answer C is incorrect.

General Police Duties, para. 4.8.6

Answer 8.8

Answer **A** — Section 114(1) of the Anti-terrorism, Crime and Security Act 2001 states that a person is guilty of an offence if he places any substance or other thing in any place or sends any substance or other thing from one place to another (by post, rail or any other means whatever) with the intention of inducing in a person anywhere in the world a belief that it is likely to be (or contain) a noxious substance or other noxious thing and thereby endanger human life or create a serious risk to human health. Answer B is incorrect as this offence is not about an intention to induce in some other person a belief the item concerned will explode or ignite. Answer D is incorrect as the intention under s. 114 is not related to causing personal injury or damage to property. The offence under s. 114(1) can be committed by sending a substance (in this case flour) by any means whatever, from one place to another, anywhere in the world. The offence is therefore committed in relation to both letters (making answer C incorrect).

General Police Duties, para. 4.8.2

Answer 8.9

Answer **D** — Answer A is incorrect as under s. 85(3) of the Postal Service Act 2000, a person commits an offence if he sends by post a postal packet which encloses:

(a) any indecent or obscene print, painting, photograph, lithograph, engraving, cinematograph film or other record of a picture or pictures, book, card or written communication, or

(b) any other indecent or obscene article (whether or not of a similar kind to those mentioned in paragraph (a)).

The intention of the person sending the article is immaterial, meaning answer C is incorrect. Answer B is incorrect as whether an article is obscene etc. is a question of fact for the court to determine in each case. That test will not look at the particular views or frailties of the recipient, but will be an objective test based on a reasonable bystander (*Kosmos Publications Ltd* v *DPP* [1975] Crim LR 345).

General Police Duties, para. 4.8.4.1

Answer 8.10

Answer **A** — Section 84 of the Postal Services Act 2000 states that it is an offence if, without reasonable excuse, a person—

(a) intentionally delays or opens a postal packet in the course of its transmission by post, or
(b) intentionally opens a mail-bag.

As soon as WALDER hides the mail-bags in the storage cupboard intending to delay the transmission of the mail (answer A) the offence is committed.

General Police Duties, para. 4.8.4

9 | Terrorism and Associated Offences

STUDY PREPARATION

The law on terrorism contained in this chapter primarily relates to the Terrorism Act 2000 and the Terrorism Act 2006.

Areas covered in this chapter include the definition of 'terrorism' and a 'terrorist' and police powers to deal with someone suspected of being one, as well as the obligations placed on members of the public to assist the authorities in identifying and dealing with terrorism. In addition, offences under the Explosive Substances Act 1883 are relevant.

QUESTIONS

Question 9.1

The police are investigating MARTINEZ, a member of an extreme animal rights group which, because of its suspected terrorist connections, has recently become a proscribed organisation in the United Kingdom.

Under s. 11 of the Terrorism Act 2000, a person commits an offence if they belong to a proscribed organisation; however, are there any circumstances under which MARTINEZ may claim a defence to this offence?

A Yes, MARTINEZ could claim that the organisation was not proscribed when she became a member.

B Yes, MARTINEZ would have to demonstrate visible evidence that she ceased to be a member of the organisation as soon as it was proscribed.

C Yes, MARTINEZ could claim that the organisation was not proscribed when she became a member *or* she has not taken part in the activities of the organisation at any time since it was proscribed.

D Yes, MARTINEZ could claim that the organisation was not proscribed when she became a member and she has not taken part in the activities of the organisation at any time since it was proscribed.

Question 9.2

GUNN is an employee of a well-known high street bank. Over the last few months she has become increasingly suspicious of a customer's account and has started to collect information which she suspects demonstrates links between the customer's account and an animal rights group. She suspects, but has no evidence, that the customer is providing money that will be used for acts of terrorism. However, she has collected information relating to his personal bank account that she suspects to be important.

In relation to disclosing her suspicions to the police, which of the following statements is correct?

A She should disclose the information as soon as it amounts to admissible evidence.

B She must disclose the information now even if it does not amount to admissible evidence.

C She should disclose only her suspicions now: the information she collected is confidential.

D There is no obligation to disclose the information: it is a matter of choice.

Question 9.3

CHARTERIS lived in a flat in London and believed that the person living in the opposite flat was a wanted terrorist. CHARTERIS's belief was based on a picture released by the police of a person who escaped after attempting to blow up a bus. CHARTERIS is too scared to contact the authorities.

Could CHARTERIS commit an offence under s. 38B(2) of the Terrorism Act 2000, by failing to disclose information about the person living in the opposite flat?

A Yes, CHARTERIS must disclose this information to a police officer as soon as reasonably practicable.

B Yes, CHARTERIS must disclose this information to a police officer or a member of Her Majesty's forces as soon as reasonably practicable.

C No, CHARTERIS did not come into possession of the information through work or employment.

D No, this offence is only committed if a person fails to disclose information about an offence involving the commission, preparation or instigation of an act of terrorism.

Question 9.4

GUL is appearing in the Divisional Court, having appealed against a conviction for encouraging acts of terrorism under s. 1(2) of the Terrorism Act 2006. The circumstances of the case were that GUL was accused of uploading videos on YouTube of scenes showing attacks on soldiers of the NATO mission in Afghanistan by members of the Taliban. GUL did not deny posting the videos, but argued that there had been no 'encouragement' in the form of words or a statement and that the videos were not depicting scenes of terrorism, since they were showing scenes of a war.

Which of the following statements is correct, in relation to the term 'encouragement', in regard to an offence under s. 1(2) of the Terrorism Act 2006?

A Communication without words or any other statement (such as posting a video) would amount to 'encouragement' under the Act and the conviction should be upheld.

B Communication without words or any other statement would amount to 'encouragement'; however, the scenes shown were not depicting scenes of terrorism.

C The defendant has not made an oral 'statement', therefore, this does not amount to 'encouragement'.

D The defendant has not made a 'statement', whether written or otherwise; therefore, this does not amount to 'encouragement'.

Question 9.5

An authorisation is in place under s. 47A of the Terrorism Act 2000. Specific intelligence has been received that a terrorist suspect is going to leave an explosive package in a busy shopping area some time today. The police have decided to evacuate the centre, but an instruction has been given to search every person on their way out of the building.

Which of the following statements is correct in relation to the utilisation of this search power by the police?

A A constable in uniform may only use this power for the purpose of discovering whether the person concerned is a terrorist.

B A constable in uniform may only use this power if he/she reasonably suspects the person concerned is a terrorist.

C A constable in uniform may only use this power if he/she reasonably suspects the search will identify evidence that the person concerned is a terrorist.

D The purpose of the search is irrelevant; once an authorisation is in place under this section, the constable in uniform may simply search any person in the area.

Question 9.6

The police have been investigating five individuals suspected of preparing for acts of terrorism, and intelligence has been received that they are in possession of bomb-making equipment. In the early hours of the morning, their address is cordoned off, following a designation under s. 33 of the Terrorism Act 2000. Officers entered the address and arrested four of the five suspects. Intelligence is received that the fifth suspect is at an address—a nearby block of four flats—which was previously unknown to the investigation team. While an arrest team is en route to the address, further intelligence is received that the fifth person is in possession of the bomb-making equipment. Inspector BENSON has contacted the operational commander, Chief Inspector CAWLEY, and asked for authorisation to cordon off the new location imme-diately. Inspector BENSON has asked that the block of flats be included in the author-isation, so that other residents may be removed from any danger presented by the bomb-making equipment.

Which of the following statements is correct, in relation to an urgent authorisa-tion under s. 33 of the Terrorism Act 2000?

A Chief Inspector CAWLEY does not have the power to make such a designation urgently, only a superintendent may do so in these circumstances.

B Inspector BENSON could make such a designation if it is required as a matter of urgency.

C The designation must be made by a superintendent, unless there are reasonable grounds to suspect that an act of terrorism is about to take place in the locality.

D Inspector BENSON could make such a designation if it is required as a matter of urgency. However, the power relates to the removal of vehicles or pedestrians and not to people in dwellings.

Question 9.7

TELLER created a home-made pipe bomb, using explosives drained from a number of fireworks, having found out how to do so on the Internet. TELLER boasted about making the pipe bomb on a social networking site and the police were informed. A warrant was executed at TELLER's house and the bomb was found. TELLER was subsequently prosecuted for an offence under s. 4 of the Explosive Substances Act 1883, but pleaded not guilty on the grounds that the bomb was made out of mere curiosity and there was no criminal intent.

What might the court take account of, when deciding whether or not TELLER was guilty of this offence?

A That the bomb was capable of being detonated.
B That the bomb was in TELLER's possession for a criminal purpose.
C That the bomb was in TELLER's possession unlawfully.
D That TELLER or some other person intended that the bomb should be detonated in some way.

Question 9.8

Information is received that there is a suspicious unattended bag left at the gateway to a park. PC HITCH (an officer in uniform) attends the scene and examines the bag from a safe distance. She is concerned about the contents of the bag and so specialist officers and equipment are called to establish its contents. Inspector SUTHERLAND (PC HITCH's supervisor) makes her way to the scene and, after being briefed by PC HITCH, considers that it would be expedient for the purposes of a terrorist investigation to designate a cordon (under the Terrorism Act 2000).

Which of the following statements is correct in respect of any such designation (under s. 34) and use of the power (under s. 36 of the Act)?

A PC HITCH would not be able to designate a cordon under any circumstances.
B Inspector SUTHERLAND may make a designation if she considers it necessary by reason of urgency.
C The powers available under s. 36 can be exercised by police officers in plain clothes.
D The maximum duration of such a designation will be 72 hours.

ANSWERS

Answer 9.1

Answer **D** — Under s. 11(1) of the Terrorism Act 2000, a person commits an offence if they belong to a proscribed organisation. It is a defence for a person charged with an offence under subsection (1) to prove:

(a) that the organisation was not proscribed on the last (or only) occasion on which he became a member or began to profess to be a member, *and*
(b) that he has not taken part in the activities of the organisation at any time while it was proscribed.

The defence is available for a person who can demonstrate *both* elements; therefore, answers A, B and C are incorrect.

General Police Duties, para. 4.9.2.1

Answer 9.2

Answer **B** — There are a number of offences contained in the Terrorism Act 2000, and some relate to money and its use for the purposes of terrorism. GUNN's suspicions about the customer's activities, if proved to be true, would amount to such an offence. Section 19 of the 2000 Act places a statutory duty on people who form a suspicion about activities they believe amount to the offences outlined here, if that belief/suspicion is based on information that comes to their attention in the course of their employment. The duty is to inform the police without delay of those suspicions, and answers A and D are therefore incorrect. They must also disclose the information on which it is based, and therefore answer C is also incorrect. Failure to comply with this duty is an offence, punishable with five years' imprisonment.

General Police Duties, para. 4.9.4.1

Answer 9.3

Answer **A** — Section 38B of the Terrorism Act 2000 states:

(1) This section applies where a person has information which he knows or believes might be of material assistance—
  (a) in preventing the commission by another person of an act of terrorism, or

(b) in securing the apprehension, prosecution or conviction of another person, in the United Kingdom, for an offence involving the commission, preparation or instigation of an act of terrorism.

A person commits an offence if he/she does not disclose the information as soon as reasonably practicable (s. 38B(2)). This would include disclosing information which would lead to the arrest of a person for an offence involving the commission, preparation or instigation of an act of terrorism, and therefore answer D is incorrect.

In England, Wales or Scotland, disclosure must be made to a constable, whereas in Northern Ireland, disclosure must be made to a constable or a member of Her Majesty's forces (s. 38B(3)). Answer B is therefore incorrect.

Section 19 of the Act places a statutory duty on people who form a suspicion about terrorism offences, based on information that comes to their attention in the course of their employment. However, this is not the case for disclosure under s. 38B. Answer C is therefore incorrect.

Note that it is a defence for a person charged with an offence under s. 38B(2) to prove that they had a reasonable excuse for not making the disclosure (s. 38B(4)).

General Police Duties, para. 4.9.4.3

Answer 9.4

Answer **A** — An offence may be committed under s. 1(2) of the Terrorism Act 2006 when a person publishes a statement to encourage the commission, preparation or instigation of acts of terrorism or Convention offences ('Convention offences' include those in relation to explosives, biological weapons, chemical weapons, nuclear weapons, hostage-taking, hijacking, terrorist funds, etc.).

Section 3(1) provides that the offence can be committed by publishing a statement electronically, i.e. via the Internet and 'statement' includes a communication of any description, including a communication without words consisting of sounds or images or both (s. 20(6)). Answers C and D are therefore incorrect.

In *R* v *Gul* [2013] UKSC 64, the defendant's conviction was upheld by the Divisional Court after he had uploaded videos on to the Internet of scenes showing attacks on soldiers of the Coalition forces in Iraq and Afghanistan by insurgents. The court held that the videos *were* depicting scenes of terrorism within the definition of s. 1 of the Terrorism Act 2000, and therefore answer B is incorrect.

General Police Duties, para. 4.9.5.1

Answer 9.5

Answer **A** — Under s. 47A of the Terrorism Act 2000, a senior police officer may give an authorisation for searches to take place in a specified area or place. An authorisation under this section authorises any constable in uniform to stop and search vehicles and pedestrians.

A constable in uniform may exercise the power conferred by an authorisation only for the purpose of discovering whether there is anything which may constitute evidence that the vehicle concerned is being used for the purposes of terrorism or (as the case may be) that the person concerned is a terrorist within the meaning of s. 40 (s. 47A(4)). Answer D is incorrect—the purpose of the search *is* relevant, it must be to discover if the person is a terrorist, or the vehicle is being used for terrorist activities.

However, the power conferred by such an authorisation may be exercised whether or not the constable reasonably suspects that there is such evidence on the person (s. 47A(5)). Answers B and C are therefore incorrect.

General Police Duties, para. 4.9.6.4

Answer 9.6

Answer **B** — Section 33 of the Terrorism Act 2000 provides the power to cordon off areas. Generally, the power to make such a designation is limited to a police officer who is of at least the rank of superintendent (s. 34(1)). However, s. 34(2) states that a constable who is not of the rank required by subs. (1) may make a designation if he considers it necessary by reason of urgency. Answer A is therefore incorrect.

Section 33(2) states that a designation may be made only if the person making it considers it expedient for the purposes of a terrorist investigation. Neither of these sections requires the authorising officer to have reasonable grounds to believe that an act of terrorism is about to take place in the locality, even if the matter is urgent, and therefore answer C is incorrect.

Section 36(1) of the Act outlines the actions a constable in uniform (or PCSO) may take in a cordoned area. They may order a person in a cordoned area to leave it immediately, order the driver or person in charge of a vehicle to move it from the area immediately, remove a vehicle in such an area or prohibit or restrict access to a cordoned area by pedestrians or vehicles. Under s. 36(1)(b) a power is given to order a person *immediately to leave premises which are wholly or partly in or adjacent to a cordoned area*. Answer D is therefore incorrect.

General Police Duties, paras 4.9.6.5 to 4.9.6.7

Answer 9.7

Answer **C** — Section 4(1) of the Explosive Substances Act 1883 states:

> Any person who makes or knowingly has in his possession or under his control any explosive substance under such circumstances as to give rise to a reasonable suspicion that he is not making it or does not have it in his possession or under his control for a lawful object, shall, unless he can show that he made it or had it in his possession or under his control for a lawful object, be guilty of a felony...

Whether a person's purpose in having the items prohibited by these offences is a 'lawful object' will need to be determined in each case (*R* v *Fegan* (1971) 78 Cr App R 189 and *R* v *G* [2009] UKHL 13).

In *R* v *Riding* [2009] EWCA Crim 892, a person alleged they had made a pipe bomb out of mere curiosity, using explosives drained from a number of fireworks. The defence contended that 'lawful object' meant the absence of a criminal purpose rather than a positive object that was lawful. However, the court was satisfied it meant the latter and mere curiosity could not be a 'lawful object' in making a lethal pipe bomb.

There is no requirement to show that the bomb was capable of being detonated, that it was in a person's possession for a criminal purpose, or that the defendant or some other person intended that the bomb should be detonated in some way. Answers A, B and D are therefore incorrect.

General Police Duties, para. 4.9.7

Answer 9.8

Answer **B** — Section 34(1)(a) of the Terrorism Act 2000 states that a designation under s. 33 (to create a cordon) may only be made by an officer of the rank of at least superintendent. However, s. 34(2) states that a constable who is not of that rank may make a designation if he/she considers it necessary by reason of urgency (making answer A incorrect and answer B correct). Section 34 provides police powers in respect of cordons but these are only available to officers in uniform, making answer C incorrect. Answer D is incorrect as the period of designation begins at the time the order is made and ends on the date specified in the order. The initial designation cannot extend beyond 14 days (s. 35(2)). However, the period during which a designation has effect may be extended in writing from time to time by the person who made it, or an officer of at least superintendent rank (s. 35(3)). There is a time limit of 28 days on extended designations and this appears to mean an overall time limit of 28 days beginning with the day on which the order is made (s. 35(5)).

General Police Duties, paras 4.9.5.5 to 4.9.5.7

10 Public Order, Processions and Assemblies

STUDY PREPARATION

This chapter addresses the maintenance of public order using the wide range of offences and powers that are available to the police. In tackling that law, it is important to know the elements of the main offences and also the features that distinguish one event from another, whether the offence is committed by an individual or by more than one person.

The long-established legislation dealing with public meetings, assemblies, demonstrations and processions is also dealt with here.

QUESTIONS

Question 10.1

DENNIS owns an off-licence and had just closed the premises late at night, locking the door. HUDSON arrived at the premises in a drunken state demanding to be let in to buy a bottle of wine. DENNIS refused to allow HUDSON in and HUDSON began shouting, 'If you don't let me in, I'll smash all these windows.' HUDSON then sat on the wall waiting for DENNIS to open the shop door.

Assuming that an arrest may be necessary in these circumstances, does DENNIS have the power to arrest HUDSON for a breach of the peace, contrary to common law?

A No, the threats were made towards DENNIS's property, not DENNIS.
B Yes, provided DENNIS reasonably believed HUDSON would carry out the threat.

C Yes, provided DENNIS reasonably believed HUDSON was capable of carrying out the threat.

D No, only a police officer has the power of arrest to prevent a breach of the peace that has not yet occurred.

Question 10.2

Constable CAREY attended a report of a domestic dispute taking place in a home. On arrival, the officer could hear sounds of a disturbance coming from inside the premises. The front door was locked and despite Constable CAREY knocking loudly several times, there was no reply.

Considering Constable CAREY's powers of entry, which of the following statements is correct?

A Constable CAREY may enter the premises to prevent a breach of the peace and to remain there in order to do so.

B Constable CAREY may enter the premises only if s. 17 of the Police and Criminal Evidence Act 1984 applies; there are no additional powers to enter to prevent a breach of the peace.

C Constable CAREY may enter the premises, provided the disturbance affected members of the public outside the property.

D Constable CAREY may enter the premises, provided the disturbance could be heard by members of the public outside the property.

Question 10.3

A group of 20 people have been charged with the offence of riot, following a serious incident of disorder on a housing estate. The Crown Prosecution Service intends introducing evidence that at least 15 of the defendants were threatening violence towards people from a minority ethnic group, while five defendants actually used violence towards them. Other evidence shows that at least ten other people were gathered near those charged. These people did not take part in the threats or violence, but their presence added to the intimidation.

According to s. 1 of the Public Order Act 1986, who can be found guilty of riot in these circumstances?

A Any of the people present who were not victims of the incident.

B Any of the defendants who used or threatened to use unlawful violence.

C The five defendants who actually used unlawful violence.

D None of the people present, as only five defendants actually used violence.

Question 10.4

HOWLEY has been charged along with a number of other people, with an offence of violent disorder, under s. 2 of the Public Order Act 1986. HOWLEY intends to use the defence that he was intoxicated at the time of the incident, and that he was not aware of his actions.

What does s. 6 of the Public Order Act 1986 state in relation to how intoxication will, if at all, impact on the charge?

A It cannot be used as a defence in relation to this offence (s. 2 violent disorder), or an offence under s. 1.

B HOWLEY may use this defence if he can show either that his intoxication was not self-induced, or it was caused solely by taking a substance in the course of medical treatment.

C HOWLEY may use this defence, but only if he can show that his intoxication was not self-induced.

D HOWLEY may use this defence, but only if he can show that his intoxication was caused solely by taking a substance in the course of medical treatment.

Question 10.5

WORTON, CAMERON and MAHROOF appeared in Crown Court for violent disorder, contrary to s. 2 of the Public Order Act 1986, following a large fight outside a pub, which was captured on CCTV. After hearing the evidence, the jury acquitted WORTON of the offence.

Could CAMERON and MAHROOF still be convicted of the offence in these circumstances?

A Yes, only two people are required to have used or threatened unlawful violence during the incident for this offence to be complete.

B No, when there are three defendants and one is acquitted of this offence, the other two defendants must also be acquitted.

C Yes, the other two defendants may still be convicted of the offence, provided it can be shown that there were three or more people using or threatening unlawful violence during the incident.

D Yes, but only if it can be shown that CAMERON and MAHROOF actually used unlawful violence (as opposed to threatening unlawful violence) during the incident.

Question 10.6

Constable CARLISLE attended a report of a stolen vehicle being driven around a housing estate. On arrival, the officer saw SALTER getting out of the stolen vehicle. Constable CARLISLE arrested SALTER, who began violently to resist arrest. While the officer was waiting for back-up, a crowd of about eight people gathered around and each of them threatened violence towards Constable CARLISLE. Some of the people then started to punch and kick the officer to aid SALTER's escape.

Has an offence of violent disorder, under s. 2 of the Public Order Act 1986, been committed in these circumstances?

A Yes, if it can be shown that the people were present together, using or threatening unlawful violence.

B Yes, but only in respect of the people who were present together, using unlawful violence.

C Yes, if it can be shown that the people were present together, using or threatening unlawful violence simultaneously.

D Yes, if it can be shown that SALTER and the other people were deliberately acting together, to use or threaten unlawful violence.

Question 10.7

WEBB and CAHILL were in dispute about a boundary between their gardens. One day, CAHILL returned from work as WEBB was about to cut down a tree, which was in the disputed boundary area. CAHILL, who owned an Alsatian dog that lived in a kennel in the rear garden, saw what was happening and shouted at WEBB, 'Stop that or I'll set the dog on you and it will cause you serious injury.' The dog was still in the kennel, but WEBB was genuinely in fear that CAHILL would carry out the threat. At the time, WEBB was alone in one enclosed garden, and CAHILL was alone in the other. There were no other people present at the scene.

Could CAHILL be guilty of an offence under s. 3 of the Public Order Act 1986 (causing an affray) in these circumstances?

A No, there was no likelihood of another person being present at the scene who would fear for their safety and the offence cannot be committed by the use of words alone.

B Yes, CAHILL threatened WEBB with immediate personal violence.

C No, CAHILL would have to threaten or use personal violence towards WEBB, rather than making a threat with the dog.

D Yes, had a person of reasonable firmness been at the scene, they would have feared for their safety.

Question 10.8

HAWKER was drunk and was standing at the bar in a busy pub waiting to be served when HUGHES appeared alongside him. A bar staff member served HUGHES before HAWKER and he became very angry, shouting at HUGHES for pushing in. HUGHES made a sarcastic comment before moving away with his drinks. HAWKER continued drinking at the bar, brooding about the incident with HUGHES. Eventually, HAWKER saw HUGHES leaving the pub and followed him outside. HAWKER came up behind HUGHES and threw a punch, intending injury to HUGHES, which completely missed, but would have caused serious injury had it connected. HAWKER was so drunk that he fell over before being able to follow up the punch. Constable DEANS was outside the pub and witnessed the incident. Because HUGHES was uninjured, the officer arrested HAWKER for an offence under s. 4 of the Public Order Act 1986.

Has Constable DEANS correctly arrested HAWKER for an offence contrary to s. 4 of the Public Order Act 1986 in these circumstances?

A No, HAWKER intended to take HUGHES by surprise, so that HUGHES would not have been aware of the assault until the act had occurred.

B No, because HUGHES did not believe that immediate and unlawful violence would be used against him.

C No, because HUGHES was not in fear that immediate and unlawful violence would be used against him.

D Yes, HAWKER intended to use immediate and unlawful violence against HUGHES.

Question 10.9

CONROY is appearing in court accused of using threatening behaviour towards Constable MERRECK, contrary to s. 4(1) of the Public Order Act 1986. CONROY has not denied using threatening behaviour, but is pleading not guilty on the grounds that the incident took place when both of them were inside a dwelling. The prosecution's solicitor has described the location of the alleged offence to the court: the incident took place in the hallway of a communal house that CONROY shares with seven other people. The hallway is accessed via a common front door, which has a digital keypad with the number restricted to the occupants. The residents have their own separate bedrooms with lockable doors and share other parts of the house, such as the lounge, kitchen and bathroom.

Would the location of the incident, as described by the prosecution's solicitor, qualify as a 'dwelling', under s. 8 of the Public Order Act 1986?

A No, where premises are shared by more than one person, no part of the structure can be classed as a dwelling as defined in s. 8.

B Yes, any part of a structure that is shared by more than one person will be classed as a dwelling as defined in s. 8.

C Yes, because the hallway could only be entered by way of a digital keypad and is restricted to the occupants, it will be classed as a dwelling as defined in s. 8.

D No, because this part of the premises is not occupied as a person's home it will not be classed as a dwelling as defined in s. 8.

Question 10.10

SADIQUE is a Ugandan Asian and has bought a product which has failed to work. He returns it to the shop and is dealt with by AKANJI, a shop assistant who is Nigerian by birth. Less than happy with the service, SADIQUE calls AKANJI 'an African twat' and 'an African bitch'. AKANJI is very distressed by this and contacts the police.

Has SADIQUE committed an offence contrary to s. 31(1)(b) of the Crime and Disorder Act 1998 (racially aggravated intentional harassment, alarm or distress)?

A No, as 'African' does not describe a racial group.

B No, as SADIQUE is from the same racial group as AKANJI.

C Yes, provided SADIQUE intended to distress AKANJI.

D Yes, there is no need to prove intent, provided distress is caused.

Question 10.11

Constable KELLEY stopped MAHER and his friend NEWTON, who were in a motor vehicle at night. Constable KELLEY had reasonable grounds to suspect they were in possession of stolen property and informed MAHER and NEWTON of his intention to search them and the vehicle. At the end of the search, which was negative, MAHER said to Constable KELLEY, 'I told you, you wouldn't fucking find anything.'

Considering the requirements of s. 5 of the Public Order Act 1986 (using threatening or abusive words or behaviour), is MAHER likely to have committed this offence?

A Yes, provided it can be shown that NEWTON heard MAHER's bad language.

B Yes, Constable KELLEY heard MAHER's bad language, which is sufficient to prove the offence.

C No, as it is unlikely that those present would have been caused any harassment, alarm or distress.

D Yes, if an innocent bystander had heard MAHER's bad language, that person may have been caused harassment, alarm or distress.

Question 10.12

Constable ROBINSON was on patrol in a shopping centre, when she saw INCE walking along, shouting and swearing in a loud voice. There were a number of shoppers in the area and Constable ROBINSON approached INCE and advised him to stop swearing and annoying people. INCE ignored Constable ROBINSON and walked away, continuing to swear loudly at passers-by. Constable ROBINSON decided that it was necessary to issue INCE with a Disorder Penalty Notice for an offence contrary to s. 5 of the Public Order Act 1986.

What would have to be proved in relation to INCE's state of mind, for the offence under s. 5 to be made out?

A That he intended his behaviour to be threatening or abusive, or was aware that it was.

B That he actually intended his behaviour to be threatening or abusive.

C That he was aware that his behaviour was threatening or abusive, whether he intended it to be so or not.

D That he ought to have been aware that his behaviour was threatening or abusive.

Question 10.13

IRWIN was treated in the casualty department of a hospital, after falling and spraining a wrist. Although the injuries were not serious, IRWIN was convinced that the arm was broken. IRWIN returned to the hospital about four hours after being discharged and insisted on receiving further treatment. IRWIN began causing a disturbance and because the hospital staff were worried about their safety, they called the police. POWELL, the on-duty security guard, became aware of the disturbance and decided to deal with IRWIN before the police arrived. POWELL was a duly authorised NHS staff member.

Would POWELL have the authority to remove IRWIN from the premises before the arrival of the police?

A No, only a constable could do so, because IRWIN was a patient, waiting for medical advice.

B Yes, either POWELL, a constable or any NHS staff member could do so, because IRWIN was not a patient, waiting for medical advice.

C Yes, either POWELL or a constable could do so, because IRWIN was not a patient, waiting for medical advice.

D No, having received treatment less than eight hours ago, IRWIN may not be ejected from the premises.

Question 10.14

A public assembly was taking place in a main thoroughfare in a city centre to demonstrate against student fees. The chief constable of the force had placed conditions in advance, as to the location and the number of people who should be present. On the day of the event, road closures were in place and the demonstration went on for 10 hours. The length of the assembly was not included in the original conditions and although the demonstration was peaceful, the police had genuine concerns over the disproportionate disruption being caused to traffic and pedestrians. As a result, the chief constable issued a further notice, authorising the demonstration to be terminated.

Were the chief constable's actions lawful in these circumstances?

A Yes, provided the chief constable was present at the assembly.

B Yes, regardless of whether the chief constable was present at the assembly.

C No, there were no conditions set as to the length of the demonstration in the original notice and the police should have allowed it to continue.

D No, there was no evidence that it was necessary to terminate the demonstration to prevent disorder, damage or intimidation.

Question 10.15

Constable JEFFERS, who is in full uniform, has been deployed to deal with a trespassory assembly, in respect of which an order under s. 14A of the Public Order Act 1986 has been obtained prohibiting it taking place. The officer is four-and-a-half miles from the historical monument where the assembly was due to take place, and is carrying out powers granted by s. 14C of the 1986 Act, preventing access to the site. Using s. 14C of the Act, the officer has stopped a vehicle, and has directed the occupants not to proceed in the direction of the assembly.

Are the officer's actions lawful?

A Yes, as the officer was in uniform the actions are lawful.

B Yes, the actions are lawful; it is immaterial that the officer was in uniform.

C No, the officer is outside the radius set by the Act at four miles.

D No, the officer has no power to stop vehicles under this section.

Question 10.16

Sergeant FOULKES attended an appointment with the chair of the local town council. A public meeting is due to be held to discuss an application to build a new housing estate on a greenfield site on the outskirts of the town. The chair had heard that a number of people were attending to protest against the application and wanted to discuss the support the council could expect from the police during the meeting if people attending became disorderly.

An offence may be committed under s. 1(1) of the Public Meeting Act 1908, if a person is disorderly at such a meeting. What powers would Sergeant FOULKES have to deal with such an offence at the meeting?

A Sergeant FOULKES may use the statutory power provided by the Act, to arrest any person reasonably suspected of committing this offence.

B Sergeant FOULKES may, if requested by the chair, remove any person reasonably suspected of committing this offence.

C Sergeant FOULKES may, if requested by the chair, require any person reasonably suspected of committing this offence to declare his/her name and address.

D Sergeant FOULKES must, if requested by the chair, remove any person reasonably suspected of committing this offence.

Question 10.17

GROSS is walking his dog in a park and allows the dog to foul near some swings where a group of children are playing and being supervised by McGUINNESS and several other adults who are all sitting on bikes. McGUINNESS is disgusted by the behaviour of GROSS allowing his dog to foul so close to where children are playing and tells him how he feels. GROSS reacts by telling McGUINNESS to 'Mind your own fuckin' business or I'll kick your head in!' McGUINNESS tells GROSS to watch his language in front of the children to which GROSS responds 'I'll set my dog on you, if you don't fuck off!' At this point, he pulls on the lead of his dog dragging it towards McGUINNESS and causing the dog to bark loudly at McGUINNESS. Several of the children start to cry and this action causes McGUINNESS and the other adults to fear for their personal safety. GROSS walks up to McGUINNESS and looks at the bike McGUINNESS is sitting on and kicks it, damaging the front wheel of the bike in the process. GROSS is thoroughly aware that his conduct from the outset is violent.

At what point, if at all, does GROSS first commit the offence of affray (contrary to s. 3 of the Public Order Act 1986)?

A When he tells McGUINNESS to 'Mind your own fuckin' business or I'll kick your head in'.

B When he says, 'I'll set my dog on you, if you don't fuck off!' and pulls the dog towards McGUINNESS.

C When he kicks the wheel of McGUINNESS's bike damaging the front wheel.

D The offence of affray has not been committed in these circumstances.

Question 10.18

In excess of 100 shoppers are waiting outside the front doors of an electrical store to get a bargain in a 'Black Friday' sale. PARKER and TURNER are right at the front of the queue as they had camped outside the shop overnight. As it gets closer to the store opening (at 09.00hrs) the crowd become agitated after some pushing and shoving led to queue-jumping. At 08.50hrs, several dozen people start chanting 'Let us in or we'll kick the door in!' At 08.55hrs, PARKER starts violently kicking the front door of the shop shouting, 'Let us in, you fuckin' twats'. Moments later, TURNER joins in by violently kicking the glass in the door of the shop shouting, 'We've been here all night so open up or I'll kick the fuckin' door off the hinges!' The manager of the store becomes concerned about the situation and, fearing for the safety of the customers, his staff and himself, he opens the shop doors letting the customers rush inside.

When, if at all, is the offence of riot (contrary to s. 1 of the Public Order Act 1986) committed?

A The offence is first committed when several dozen people start chanting 'Let us in or we'll kick the door in!'

B The offence is first committed when PARKER starts violently kicking the door frame of the shop shouting 'Let us in, you fuckin' twats!'

C The offence is first committed when TURNER starts violently kicking the glass in the door shouting, 'We've been here all night so open up or I'll kick the fuckin' door off the hinges!'

D The offence of riot has not been committed in these circumstances.

ANSWERS

Answer 10.1

Answer **B** — A breach of the peace was defined specifically in *R* v *Howell* [1982] QB 416. A breach of the peace generally occurs when an act is done, or threatened to be done:

- which harms a person or, in his/her presence, his/her property; or
- which is likely to cause such harm; or
- which puts someone in fear of such harm.

Since DENNIS was in fear that harm would be done to the shop, answer A is incorrect.

A constable or any other person may arrest without warrant any person:

- who is committing a breach of the peace;
- whom he/she reasonably believes will commit a breach of the peace in the immediate future; or
- who has committed a breach of the peace, where it is reasonably believed that a recurrence of the breach of the peace is threatened.

The power of arrest is given to a constable or any other person (answer D is therefore incorrect). There is no requirement for the person to reasonably believe that the other person is capable of carrying out the threat, merely that the threat may be carried out. Answer C is incorrect.

General Police Duties, paras 4.10.2, 4.10.2.4

Answer 10.2

Answer **A** — A breach of the peace may take place on private premises as well as in public places (*R* v *Chief Constable of Devon and Cornwall, ex parte Central Electricity Generating Board* [1982] QB 458) and the police are entitled to enter premises to prevent a breach of the peace and to remain there in order to do so (*Thomas* v *Sawkins* [1935] 2 KB 249).This power is not affected by the general powers of entry provided by s. 17 of the Police and Criminal Evidence Act 1984—it is an additional power and answer B is incorrect.

Although the courts have declared that the presence of a member (or members) of the public is a highly relevant factor when dealing with a breach of the peace (*McConnell* v *Chief Constable of Greater Manchester Police* [1990] 1 WLR 364), it has also been held that if a breach of the peace takes place on private property, there is no requirement to show that the resulting disturbance affected members of the public outside that property (*McQuade* v *Chief Constable of Humberside Police* [2001] EWCA Civ 1330). Answers C and D are therefore incorrect.

General Police Duties, para. 4.10.2.1

Answer 10.3

Answer **C** — Under s. 1(1) of the Public Order Act 1986:

Where 12 or more persons who are present together use or threaten unlawful violence for a common purpose and the conduct of them (taken together) is such as would cause a person of reasonable firmness present at the scene to fear for his personal safety, each of the persons using unlawful violence for the common purpose is guilty of riot.

The offence of riot may be made out in these circumstances against the five defendants who actually used violence (answer D is therefore incorrect). However, only those defendants who actually used violence will be guilty, and therefore answers A and B are incorrect. Of course, other defendants present may also be guilty of other serious Public Order Act offences.

General Police Duties, para. 4.10.3

Answer 10.4

Answer **B** — Section 6(5) of the Public Order Act 1986 states:

For the purposes of this section a person whose awareness is impaired by intoxication shall be taken to be aware of that of which he would be aware if not intoxicated, unless he shows either that his intoxication was not self-induced or that it was caused solely by the taking or administration of a substance in the course of medical treatment.

The defence under s. 6(5) applies to all of the general Public Order Act offences; therefore, answer A is incorrect.

The defence may be raised either when the defendant claims intoxication was not self-induced or that it was caused solely by the taking or administration of a substance in the course of medical treatment. Answers C and D are therefore incorrect.

General Police Duties, para. 4.10.3.2

Answer 10.5

Answer **C** — Section 2(1) of the Public Order Act 1986 states:

> Where 3 or more persons who are present together use or threaten unlawful violence and the conduct of them (taken together) is such as would cause a person of reasonable firmness present at the scene to fear for his personal safety, each of the persons using or threatening unlawful violence is guilty of violent disorder.

Section 2(1) requires that *three* or more persons were present together who used or threatened unlawful violence, and therefore answer A is incorrect.

In order to convict any defendant of this offence, it must be shown that there were three or more people using or threatening violence. However, where two of the defendants are acquitted, the remaining defendant can still be convicted (*R* v *Mahroof* (1989) 88 Cr App R 317) as long as it can be proved that there *were* three or more people using or threatening violence (perhaps from CCTV evidence of the incident). If it cannot be proved that there were three or more people using or threatening unlawful violence, the court should acquit each defendant (*R* v *McGuigan* [1991] Crim LR 719). Therefore, answer B is incorrect.

For an offence of riot, under s. 1 of the Act, only the persons who actually used violence may be convicted. This is not the case for an offence under s. 2; therefore, answer D is incorrect.

General Police Duties, para. 4.10.4

Answer 10.6

Answer **A** — Under s. 2(1) of the Public Order Act 1986, where three or more persons who are present together use or threaten unlawful violence and the conduct of them (taken together) is such as would cause a person of reasonable firmness present at the scene to fear for their personal safety, each of the persons using or threatening unlawful violence is guilty of violent disorder. Unlike the offence of riot (under s. 1 of the Act), for this offence each of the persons using *or* threatening unlawful violence may be guilty of the offence; therefore, answer B is incorrect.

Under s. 2, there is no requirement to show that the persons using or threatening unlawful violence did so simultaneously (unlike the offence under s. 1), and therefore answer C is incorrect.

The circumstances in this question are similar to the case of *R* v *NW* [2010] EWCA Crim 404. In that case, a person was violently resisting arrest by a police officer, during which time a crowd gathered and various members of the crowd used or threatened violence. The Court of Appeal held that for the purposes of this section, it was not necessary for a person to deliberately act in combination with at least two other people present at the scene, but that it is sufficient that at least three people be present, each separately using or threatening unlawful violence. Answer D is therefore incorrect.

General Police Duties, para. 4.10.4

Answer 10.7

Answer **A** — Under s. 3(1) of the Public Order Act 1986, a person is guilty of affray if he/she uses or threatens unlawful violence towards another and his/her conduct is such as would cause a person of reasonable firmness present at the scene to fear for his/her personal safety.

However, in order to prove this offence, the threat cannot be made by words alone (s. 3(3)). CAHILL has not committed an act of violence towards WEBB (either personally or with the dog) in these circumstances as the behaviour merely amounted to a verbal threat. Answer B is therefore incorrect.

The 'action' by the defendant *may* consist of utilising something else such as a dog to threaten the violence (*R* v *Dixon* [1993] Crim LR 579). Answer C is therefore incorrect.

Finally, for this offence to be complete, the House of Lords has held that, in order to prove the offence of affray, the threat of unlawful violence has to be towards a person (or persons) present at the scene (*I* v *DPP* [2001] UKHL 10). This means that there does have to be *someone* other than the defendant at the scene.

Once this element has been proved, it will be necessary to prove the second element, namely whether the defendant's conduct would have caused a hypothetical person present at the scene to fear for his/her personal safety (*R* v *Sanchez* (1996) 160 JP 321 and *R* v *Carey* [2006] EWCA Crim 17).

However, where the likelihood of a hypothetical person of reasonable firmness being present was low this element of the offence was not satisfied. In *R (On the Application of Leeson)* v *DPP* [2010] EWHC 994 (Admin), a woman had issued a drunken threat to kill her long-term partner whilst holding a knife, in a bathroom, in an otherwise unoccupied house. In these circumstances the court held that there was no possibility of a hypothetical bystander fearing for their safety.

The most recent case (*Leeson* noted previously) places a different perspective on the 'hypothetical' third person, and in the example given in this question, the two parties were in separate enclosed gardens, with very little likelihood of another person being affected by the behaviour (as opposed to a situation in a pub, for example, where several people could be injured). This makes answer A correct, and answer D incorrect.

General Police Duties, para. 4.10.5

Answer 10.8

Answer **A** — Under s. 4(1) of the Public Order Act 1986:

A person is guilty of an offence if he/she—
(a) uses towards another person threatening, abusive or insulting words or behaviour, or
(b) distributes or displays to another person any writing, sign or other visible representation which is threatening, abusive or insulting,
with intent to cause that person to believe that immediate unlawful violence will be used against him or another by any person, or to provoke the immediate use of unlawful violence by that person or another, or whereby that person is likely to believe that such violence will be used or it is likely that such violence will be provoked.

Under s. 6(3) of the Act, a person is guilty of an offence only if he/she *intends* his/her words or behaviour to be threatening, abusive or insulting, or is aware that they may be. It is HAWKER's intent that counts, not whether HUGHES actually believed or even feared that immediate unlawful violence would be used against him. Answers B and C are therefore incorrect.

It is not possible to prove that the victim feared immediate unlawful violence, where it was the intention of the accused to take the victim by surprise so that they did not know they would be assaulted until the act had occurred. The court considered that the accused should have been charged with assault (*Hughes* v *DPP* [2012] EWHC 606 (Admin)). This case shows that if HAWKER simply intended to use immediate and unlawful violence against HUGHES without the required threats, the offence is not made out, and therefore answer D is incorrect.

General Police Duties, para. 4.10.6

Answer 10.9

Answer **D** — An offence under s. 4(2) of the Public Order Act 1986 may be committed in a public or private place. However, no offence will be committed where the words or behaviour are used, or the writing, sign or other visible representation is distributed or displayed, by a person inside a dwelling and the other person is also inside that or another dwelling.

Section 8 of the Public Order Act 1986 provides the definition of a dwelling, which is:

any structure or part of a structure occupied as a person's home or as other living accommodation (whether the occupation is separate or shared with others) but does not include any part not so occupied, and for this purpose 'structure' includes a tent, caravan, vehicle, vessel or other temporary or movable structure.

Therefore, it is not correct to say that where premises are shared by more than one person, no part of the structure can be classed as a dwelling. Living accommodation (such as a person's bedroom) will fall within the definition in s. 8, whether the occupation is separate or shared with others. Answer A is therefore incorrect.

On the other hand, it is also not correct to state that any part of a structure that is shared by more than one person will be classed as a dwelling as defined in s. 8. Even where accommodation is shared, any part of the premises not used as 'living accommodation' will not be classed as a dwelling. Answer B is therefore incorrect.

In *Le Vine* v *DPP* [2010] EWHC 1128 (Admin), a laundry room, commonly used by tenants in sheltered housing, did not form part of a dwelling. Similarly, communal landings which form access routes to separate dwellings have been held not to constitute part of a dwelling even though they could only be entered by way of an entryphone system (*Rukwira* v *DPP* [1993] Crim LR 882). Answer C is therefore incorrect.

Note that a police cell has been held not to be living accommodation for the purposes of s. 8 (*R* v *Francis* [2006] EWCA Crim 3323).

General Police Duties, para. 4.10.6.1

Answer 10.10

Answer **C** — This question loosely follows the circumstances of *R* v *White (Anthony Delroy)* [2001] 1 WLR 1352, where the Court of Appeal upheld White's conviction for this offence. The court held that the words used are to be construed as they are generally used in England and Wales; and on that basis the word 'African' described a racial group defined by reference to race, and therefore answer A is incorrect. This offence can be committed towards people from the same racial group as the accused, and answer B is therefore incorrect. This is a crime of 'specific intent' and as such does require the intent to be proven, and therefore answer D is incorrect.

General Police Duties, para. 4.10.7

Answer 10.11

Answer **C** — The Public Order Act 1986, s. 5 states:

A person is guilty of an offence if he—
(a) uses threatening or abusive words or behaviour, or disorderly behaviour, or
(b) displays any writing, sign or other visible representation which is threatening or abusive, within the hearing or sight of a person likely to be caused harassment, alarm or distress thereby.

There needs to be a person within whose sight or hearing the conduct takes place. This requirement was confirmed in *Taylor* v *DPP* [2006] EWHC 1202 (Admin), where it was held that there must be at least evidence that there was someone who could see, or could hear, at the material time, what the individual was doing. It would not be sufficient to show that an 'innocent bystander' may have been caused harassment, alarm or distress; there was no such person present and answer D is therefore incorrect.

The second element that has to be proved is that any of the people present were *likely* to have been caused harassment, alarm or distress by the defendant's conduct. In *Harvey* v *DPP* [2011] EWHC Crim B1 (Admin), the defendant had used bad language when detained by the police (saying, e.g., 'I told you, you wouldn't find fuck all') and although this might have been considered abusive, there was no evidence that anyone involved, or any bystanders, had suffered or were likely to have been caused any harassment, alarm or distress. All those involved would have heard such language on many occasions and in consequence the Appeal Court quashed the conviction. Of course, each case will be different, but using the *Harvey* case as an example, it is likely that even if NEWTON had overheard the swearing, he would not have been caused harassment, alarm or distress by the words used by MAHER. The same would be the case in respect of Constable KELLEY and for that reason answers A and B are incorrect.

General Police Duties, para. 4.10.8

Answer 10.12

Answer **A** — Section 6 of the Public Order Act 1986 states that a person is guilty of an offence under s. 5 only if:

> he intends his words or behaviour, or the writing, sign or other visible representation, to be threatening or abusive, or is aware that it may be threatening or abusive, or (as the case may be) he intends his behaviour to be or is aware that it may be disorderly.

This is not an offence which relies only on the intent of the person exhibiting the behaviour; it can also be committed if a person is simply aware that their behaviour is threatening or abusive. Answer B is therefore incorrect. This is also a case of either/or: INCE would either have to intend his behaviour to be threatening or abusive, or he would have to be aware that it was; therefore, answer C is incorrect.

The fact that a person ought to have known that his/her behaviour was threatening or abusive is immaterial, making answer D incorrect. The person's state of mind is often ignored when it comes to charging people with offences under s. 5 (and s. 4). Occasionally, defence solicitors make a point of insisting that their client be interviewed before charge. While it may be impractical to interview all offenders for these offences, it may be worth considering when the facts are unclear.

General Police Duties, para. 4.10.8.1

Answer 10.13

Answer **C** — Section 119(1) of the Criminal Justice and Immigration Act 2008 creates an offence of causing a nuisance or disturbance to an NHS staff member who is working on NHS premises and then failing to leave when required to do so by a constable or an NHS staff member. This section will only apply to people who are not on the NHS premises for the purpose of obtaining medical advice, treatment or care for themselves.

Section 120 of the 2008 Act provides a power for a constable or authorised person to remove a person who has committed an offence under s. 119. Although a non-authorised NHS staff member may ask a person to leave, this does not extend to a power of removal of a person who refuses. Answer B is therefore incorrect.

An authorised officer cannot remove the person if it is reasonably believed they are in need of medical advice etc. or that such removal would endanger their mental or physical health (s. 120(4)). However, a person ceases to be on NHS premises for the purpose of obtaining medical advice, treatment or care for himself or herself in the following two circumstances:

- once the person has received the medical advice (s. 119(3)(a));
- if the person has received the medical advice etc. during the last eight hours (s. 119(3)(b)).

Having received treatment less than eight hours previously, IRWIN is not a patient and may be ejected from the premises. Answers A and D are therefore incorrect.

General Police Duties, para. 4.10.9

Answer 10.14

Answer **A** — Under s. 14(1) of the Public Order Act 1986, if the senior police officer, having regard to the time or place at which and the circumstances in which any public assembly is being held or is intended to be held, reasonably believes that:

(a) it may result in serious public disorder, serious damage to property or serious disruption to the life of the community, or

(b) the purpose of the persons organising it is the intimidation of others with a view to compelling them not to do an act they have a right to do, or to do an act they have a right not to do,

he or she may give directions imposing on the persons organising or taking part in the assembly such conditions as to the place at which the assembly may be (or continue to be) held, its maximum duration, or the maximum number of persons who may constitute it, as appear to him/her necessary to prevent such disorder, damage, disruption or intimidation.

Section 14(1) allows for the police to react to the prevailing circumstances during the assembly; therefore, even though no conditions were set in advance as to the length of the demonstration, provided it appeared necessary to prevent disorder, damage, disruption or intimidation, it was lawful to impose further conditions while the demonstration was being held. Answer C is therefore incorrect.

A direction under s. 14(1) was lawful where a senior police officer imposed a condition that a Climate Camp protest against the G20 Summit in London must stop. The demonstration had lasted the best part of 12 hours and the court held this was quite long enough for the protestors to take advantage of their human rights under Art. 10 (Freedom of Expression) and Art. 11 (Freedom of Assembly and Association) and those wishing to remain were intent on continuing to block the highway, the main thoroughfare into and out of the City. There was no justification to prolong the demonstration and its continuation would cause serious disturbances and disruption to traffic and pedestrians wishing to use the highway. The police had a duty to clear the highway and that could not be done without removing the protestors by force if necessary (*R (On the Application of Moos)* v *Commissioner of Police of the Metropolis* [2011] EWHC 957 (Admin)). Serious disruption is included in this section and answer D is incorrect.

Finally, under s. 14(2), 'the senior police officer' means:

(a) in relation to an assembly being held, the most senior in rank of the police officers present at the scene, and
(b) in relation to an assembly intended to be held, the chief officer of police.

This means that in advance of the assembly, the chief constable was the appropriate officer to impose conditions; however, once it had commenced, any further conditions must be imposed by the senior police officer present at the scene (*R v Lucas* (2014) 17 April (not reported)), where the notice under s. 14 was signed by a chief officer who was not present at the scene, making it invalid). Answer B is therefore incorrect.

General Police Duties, para. 4.10.10.4

Answer 10.15

Answer **D** — Under s. 14A of the Public Order Act 1986, the chief officer of police has the power, if he/she reasonably believes that it is intended to hold a trespassory assembly which may result in serious disruption to the life of the community or significant damage to land or a building or monument which is of historical, archaeological or scientific importance, to apply to the district council for an order prohibiting for a specified period the holding of all trespassory assemblies in the district or part of it. The order must not last for more than four days and must not apply to an area greater than that represented by a circle of five miles radius from a specified centre, and therefore answer C is incorrect. A constable, who must be in uniform, has power to stop someone he/she reasonably believes to be on his/her way to an assembly prohibited by an order under s. 14A and to direct him/her not to proceed in the direction of the assembly, and therefore answer B is incorrect. This power, however, does not apply to vehicles and is restricted to 'stop that person', and answer A is therefore incorrect. Other powers exist to stop the vehicle, however.

General Police Duties, paras 4.10.10.5, 4.10.10.6

Answer 10.16

Answer **C** — Section 1 of the Public Meeting Act 1908 states:

(1) Any person who at a lawful public meeting acts in a disorderly manner for the purpose of preventing the transaction of the business for which the meeting was called together shall be guilty of an offence and shall on summary conviction be liable to imprisonment for a term not exceeding six months or to a fine not exceeding £1,000 or to both...

(2) Any person who incites others to commit an offence under this section shall be guilty of a like offence.

If a constable reasonably suspects any person of committing this offence, he/she *may*, if requested by the person chairing the meeting, require the offender to *declare his/her name and address immediately*. Failing to comply with such a request or giving false details is a summary offence (s. 1(3)). Answers B and D are incorrect.

There is no statutory power of arrest provided by the 1908 Act; therefore, answer A is incorrect. Of course, if the person fails to give their name and address, the arrest may be necessary under s. 24 of the Police and Criminal Evidence Act 1984.

General Police Duties, para. 4.10.10.7

Answer 10.17

Answer **B** — Section 3 of the Public Order Act 1986 states:

(1) A person is guilty of affray if he uses or threatens unlawful violence towards another and his conduct is such as would cause a person of reasonable firmness present at the scene to fear for his personal safety.

A threat cannot be made by the use of words alone (s. 3(3)) which means that answer A is incorrect. There must be some action by the defendant—even if that 'action' consists of utilising something else such as a dog to threaten the violence (*R v Dixon* [1993] Crim LR 579). So in using the dog, the offence of affray has been committed, meaning that answer D is incorrect. 'Violence' does not include violence towards property so the offence would not be committed by the actions of GROSS at answer C.

General Police Duties, para. 4.10.5

Answer 10.18

Answer **B** — Section 1(1) of the Public Order Act 1986 states that where 12 or more persons who are present together use or threaten unlawful violence for a common purpose and the conduct of them (taken together) is such as would cause a person of reasonable firmness present at the scene to fear for his personal safety, each of the persons using unlawful violence for the common purpose is guilty of riot. An important point to note is that it is only the persons *using* violence who can be guilty of the offence of riot. 'Violence' is defined under s. 8 of the Public Order Act 1986 and at s. 8(a) it states that 'violence' will include violent conduct against property as well as violent conduct towards persons (except in the context of affray). So the first few ingredients for a potential riot situation would require 12 or more persons present together (you have that number and more outside the shop) using or threatening violence (the threats by the crowd and also the use of violence on property by PARKER and TURNER) for a common purpose (getting into the shop). However, only those using violence commit the offence and the point at which violence is *first* used is when PARKER violently kicks the door of the shop so the correct answer is B.

General Police Duties, paras 4.10.3 to 4.10.3.1

11 | Sporting Events

STUDY PREPARATION

The maintenance of public order at sporting events is an important area of responsibility for the police. Large sporting events can tie up significant numbers of officers and the emphasis today is on more preventative measures to control spectators.

The Sporting Events (Control of Alcohol etc.) Act 1985 and the Football (Offences) Act 1991 create offences relating to drunkenness and rowdy behaviour at designated sporting events, while the Football Spectators Act 1989 provides the courts with significant powers to issue banning orders against those who are involved with football-related disorder, in connection with regulated football matches both inside and outside the United Kingdom.

QUESTIONS

Question 11.1

The police were working at a designated football match when, at half time, a complaint was received that away fans had been engaged in racialist chanting during the first half. Stewards and the police viewed CCTV and played back images of away supporters shouting, 'You're just a town full of Pakis' at the home fans. They managed to identify the area of the ground where the chanting was coming from and extra stewards and officers were posted to take action if needed.

Considering the offence under s. 3(1) of the Football (Offences) Act 1991 ('racialist' chanting), which of the following statements is correct?

A The prosecution would need to show that the chanting might have been racialist in its nature.

B   The prosecution would need to show that the chanting was racialist in its nature.

C   The prosecution would need to show that the chanting may have been perceived as being racialist in its nature by the people it was directed at.

D   The prosecution would need to show that the away fans intended the chanting to be racialist in its nature.

Question 11.2

The police have been looking for JENSEN to serve a notice on him prior to applying for a banning order against him, because of his violent behaviour at Premiership football matches. JENSEN has so far evaded the police; however, officers working at a home tie of a UEFA Champions League match have been circulated his photograph. JENSEN is spotted outside the ground at the end of the game by Constable BARNETT and because the next game for the club is in two weeks' time, which is the return leg abroad, the officer is keen to detain JENSEN before he disappears again.

Would Constable BARNETT be entitled to detain JENSEN in these circumstances, using powers under s. 21A(2) of the Football Spectators Act 1989?

A   No, there is no power of detention at this time because this is not within the control period.

B   Yes, JENSEN could be detained for up to a maximum of six hours while a decision is being made whether to serve a notice on him.

C   No, JENSEN has not yet been served with a notice outlining that a banning order is to be applied for.

D   Yes, JENSEN could be detained for up to a maximum of four hours while a decision is being made whether to serve a notice on him.

Question 11.3

HUNTER was driving a public service vehicle containing a number of passengers who support an English Premier League club. HUNTER was driving the supporters home from a match against another Premier League club. The vehicle was stopped on the motorway by the police, who found that many of the passengers were either in possession of alcohol or drunk. HUNTER admitted stopping at a shop, to allow the passengers to buy alcohol, which they brought onto the vehicle.

Which of the following statements is correct, in relation to offences that may have been committed under the Sporting Events (Control of Alcohol etc.) Act 1985?

A   No offences were committed under this Act, as the supporters were not on their way to a designated sporting event.

B HUNTER committed the offence, along with anyone who was drinking alcohol in the vehicle.

C HUNTER committed the offence, along with anyone who was drunk in the vehicle.

D HUNTER committed the offence, along with anyone who was in possession of alcohol or who was drunk in the vehicle.

Question 11.4

GITTENS was involved in an accident while driving to a Premier League football match, which was due to commence in three hours. GITTENS had managed to obtain a distress flare, which was in the car at the time of the accident. Constable MAY attended the scene and whilst dealing with the accident, the officer saw the flare on the front passenger seat of the car. GITTENS admitted to Constable MAY that he was intending to smuggle it into the ground.

Would Constable MAY be able to deal with GITTENS in relation to the flare, under s. 2A of the Sporting Events (Control of Alcohol etc.) Act 1985?

A No, it was outside the period of a designated sporting event.

B Yes, GITTENS was in possession of an article whose main purpose is the emission of a flare.

C Yes, GITTENS had with him an article whose main purpose is the emission of a flare.

D No, GITTENS was not at a designated sports ground, or trying to enter one.

Question 11.5

WINGROVE supports a football team which is a member of the English Premier League, which has qualified for the Champions League. WINGROVE has managed to buy 50 tickets for an away game in Germany (classed as a 'designated football match') and has advertised them for sale on a website. WINGROVE intends making a profit by selling the tickets at more than their market value.

Does WINGROVE commit an offence under s. 166 of the Criminal Justice and Public Order Act 1994, in these circumstances?

A No, the offence does not apply to football matches abroad.

B No, the offence will only be committed when WINGROVE actually sells a ticket.

C No, the offence only applies to international football matches abroad.

D Yes, provided WINGROVE is not authorised by the organisers of the match.

ANSWERS

Answer 11.1

Answer **B** — It is an offence under s. 3(1) of the Football (Offences) Act 1991 to engage or take part in chanting of an indecent or racialist nature at a designated football match.

Section 3(2) goes on to describe the meaning of 'chanting' and 'racialist':

(a) 'chanting' means the repeated uttering of any words or sounds (whether alone or in concert with one or more others); and

(b) 'of a racialist' nature means consisting of or including matter which is threatening, abusive or insulting to a person by reason of his colour, race, nationality (including citizenship) or ethnic or national origins.

The wording of s. 3(2)(b) requires that the chanting *is*, rather than *might be*, threatening, abusive or insulting. Answer A is therefore incorrect.

One way to prove this element of the offence would be the evidence of a person who was threatened, abused or insulted, but this is not expressly required in the Act (and answer C is incorrect). The court is able to make a judgment for itself, for example in *DPP* v *Stoke on Trent Magistrates' Court* [2003] EWHC 1593 (Admin) it was held that shouting 'You're just a town full of Pakis' at supporters from Oldham fell squarely within the definition.

There is no requirement for the prosecution to show that the defendants intended the chanting to be racialist in its nature; they would simply need to demonstrate that it was racialist. Answer D is therefore incorrect.

General Police Duties, para. 4.11.3

Answer 11.2

Answer **A** — The Football Spectators Act 1989, s. 21A states:

(1) This section and section 21B below apply during any control period in relation to a regulated football match outside the United Kingdom or an external tournament if a constable in uniform—

(a) has reasonable grounds for suspecting that the condition in section 14B(2) above is met in the case of a person present before him, and

(b) has reasonable grounds to believe that making a banning order in his case would help to prevent violence or disorder at or in connection with any regulated football matches ...

(2) The constable may detain the person in his custody (whether there or elsewhere) until he has decided whether or not to issue a notice under section 21B, and shall give the person his reasons for detaining him in writing.

The condition referred to in s. 21A(1)(a) is that the person has at any time caused or contributed to any violence or disorder in the United Kingdom or elsewhere.

Answer C is incorrect as there is no requirement to serve a notice on a person *before* detaining them under s. 21A(2). The actual purpose of the power is to detain a person in order to decide whether or not to serve a notice of a banning order on him/her.

A person may not be detained under subs. (2) for more than four hours or, with the authority of an officer of at least the rank of inspector, six hours (s. 21A(3)). Therefore, the *maximum* period of detention while deciding whether or not to serve the notice is six hours and answer D is incorrect.

Finally, both answers B and D are also incorrect because the power under s. 21A(2) is only applicable during any control period in relation to a regulated football match outside the United Kingdom or an external tournament. 'Control period' means, in relation to a regulated football match outside England and Wales, the period:

- before the day of the match, and
- ending when the match is finished or cancelled.

This means there is no power to detain JENSEN at this time; however, the opportunity to do so will come before the next game for the club, in the five-day period leading up to the second leg.

General Police Duties, para. 4.11.4.4

Answer 11.3

Answer **D** — Section 1 of the Sporting Events (Control of Alcohol etc.) Act 1985 applies to people who are being conveyed in public service vehicles or railway passenger vehicles, which are being used for the principal purpose of carrying passengers to *or from* designated sporting events (s. 1(1)). Answer A is therefore incorrect.

Under s. 1(2), a person who knowingly causes or permits alcohol to be carried on a vehicle to which the section applies is guilty of an offence (which makes HUNTER guilty of the offence). Other offences are committed by any person who has alcohol in his/her possession while on a vehicle to which this section applies (s. 1(3)), or to a person who is drunk on such a vehicle (s. 1(3)). Since the offence applies to both classes of people, answer C is incorrect.

Section 1 does not actually mention people who are *drinking* alcohol whilst in a vehicle to which this section applies (although by implication, such people are likely to be in possession of alcohol). Since the wording is incorrect (and the offence applies both to people who have alcohol in their possession *and* who are drunk), answer B is incorrect.

General Police Duties, para. 4.11.5

Answer 11.4

Answer **D** — Under s. 2A(1) of the Sporting Events (Control of Alcohol etc.) Act 1985, a person is guilty of an offence if he/she has an article or substance to which this section applies in his/her possession:

(a) at any time during the period of a designated sporting event when he is in any area of a designated sports ground from which the event may be directly viewed, or
(b) while entering or trying to enter a designated sports ground at any time during the period of a designated sporting event at the ground.

Articles include distress flares, smoke bombs, fumigators and fireworks.

However, the offence is not committed when the person is on his/her way to the ground (whether it is inside or outside the period of a designated sporting event). Answers A, B and C are therefore incorrect.

Note that the offence can be committed by being in 'possession' of the article, a broader concept than 'having with him'.

General Police Duties, para. 4.11.5.4

Answer 11.5

Answer **D** — It is an offence under s. 166(1) of the Criminal Justice and Public Order Act 1994 for an unauthorised person to sell a ticket for a designated football match, or otherwise to dispose of such a ticket to another person. A person is 'unauthorised' unless he/she is authorised in writing to sell or otherwise dispose of tickets for the match by the organisers of the match (s. 166(2)(a)).

Section 166(2)(aa) outlines the criteria for 'selling' a ticket, which include offering to sell a ticket, exposing a ticket for sale and advertising that a ticket is available for purchase. Answer B is therefore incorrect.

As the game concerned is a 'designated football match', answers A and C are therefore incorrect.

General Police Duties, para. 4.11.6

12 | Weapons

STUDY PREPARATION

While the definition contained in s. 1 of the Prevention of Crime Act 1953 is helpful, you need to know the component parts to fully understand the offence. Learn the meaning of 'lawful authority', 'reasonable excuse', 'has with him' and 'public place'; there are many decided cases to assist you. You must also, of course, learn the three categories of offensive weapons.

Also, you must be able to tell the difference between an 'offensive weapon' and a 'weapon of offence', as contained in the offence of trespassing with a weapon of offence, under the Criminal Law Act 1977. The manufacture and sale of weapons receive attention, with a long list of weapons that may not be manufactured or sold, etc. Further offences may be committed by selling and marketing knives and articles to children under 16.

QUESTIONS

Question 12.1

VAUGHAN ordered a novelty item over the Internet, which was delivered directly to his house. The item was a flick-knife which could also be operated as a cigarette lighter. VAUGHAN did not take the flick-knife out of the house, but regularly brought it out to show his friends when they came round.

Considering that the article could be an offensive weapon, which of the following statements is correct, according to s. 1(1) of the Prevention of Crime Act 1953?

A The article is an offensive weapon *per se* and VAUGHAN is guilty of the offence in these circumstances.

B The article is not an offensive weapon *per se*, but VAUGHAN could be guilty of the offence if he intended to use it as one.

C The article is an offensive weapon *per se*, but VAUGHAN is not guilty of the offence in these circumstances.

D The article is not an offensive weapon *per se*, but it has been adapted to be one and VAUGHAN could be guilty of the offence in these circumstances.

Question 12.2

AITKEN had recently split up from SPENCER as a result of suffering serious domestic abuse. She had moved into sheltered accommodation and was living anonymously in a different city. She had managed to secure a job in a bar, which meant she finished work late at night. AITKEN had received a phone call from a friend who told her that SPENCER had found out the area she was living in and to be careful. AITKEN believed that SPENCER was resourceful enough to find her and started carrying a knife in her bag for her own protection and would have used it for self-defence, fearing an imminent attack by her ex-partner.

With these circumstances in mind, which of the following statements is correct, in relation to having a reasonable excuse for having an offensive weapon in a public place?

A Carrying a knife for your own protection will not amount to a reasonable excuse; AITKEN would commit this offence in these circumstances.

B Carrying a knife for your protection may amount to a reasonable excuse provided the person believed he/she was at risk of an imminent attack, and the belief was reasonable.

C Having an offensive weapon with you for self-defence may amount to a reasonable excuse, provided you have armed yourself instantaneously, e.g. immediately prior to an attack.

D Carrying a knife as a general precaution that you may be attacked may amount to a reasonable excuse provided the person believed he/she was at risk of an attack at some time in the future.

Question 12.3

FAWCETT was driving home from work when he caused another car, being driven by GRANT, to brake sharply. GRANT followed him, shouting obscenities and sounding his horn. When FAWCETT stopped at traffic lights, GRANT got out of his car and ran towards him. FAWCETT got out of his own car and picked up a steering wheel lock, and threw it at GRANT, intending to injure him.

Is the steering wheel lock an 'offensive weapon' in these circumstances?

A No, FAWCETT formed the intention to use the article after it came into his possession.

B Yes, as soon as FAWCETT formed the intention to use the article.

C Yes, because FAWCETT used the article, intending to injure GRANT.

D Yes, as soon as FAWCETT picked the article up with the intention to use it.

Question 12.4

Constable BAKER was on patrol when she stopped a vehicle owned and being driven by CLEMENT. HARVEY was in the front passenger seat. Constable BAKER made a search of the vehicle and discovered a flick-knife in the glove compartment.

Could HARVEY and CLEMENT be guilty of an offence under the Prevention of Crime Act 1953?

A No, only CLEMENT may commit the offence, being the owner of the car.

B Yes, the offence is complete against both; no further proof is required.

C No, it is not possible for two people to have the same weapon with them.

D Yes, provided they both knew that the other person had it with him at the time.

Question 12.5

PENFOLD was stopped and searched on his way to a football match while he was walking in High Street. The searching officer, Constable MARRIOTT, discovered in PENFOLD's pocket a number of 50 pence pieces that had been sharpened around the edges. Believing that they were offensive weapons, the officer lawfully arrested PENFOLD.

In order to prove that PENFOLD was guilty of possessing an offensive weapon would Constable MARRIOTT need to prove intent by PENFOLD to use the coins to cause injury?

A No, provided it can be shown that the coins have been made to cause injury.

B Yes, because there is no apparent victim in these circumstances.

C Yes, because the coins are not offensive weapons *per se*.

D No, provided it can be shown the coins have been adapted to cause injury.

Question 12.6

Constable BRADY stopped and searched CLOUGH in a park one evening, after receiving information that he was carrying a knife. Constable BRADY found a folding knife with a blade of approximately 3.5 inches in length, in CLOUGH's pocket. CLOUGH claimed that he was a scout and bought the knife from a camping shop and it was intended for cutting string.

Which of the following statements is correct, in relation to the knife that Constable BRADY found?

A The knife could be an offensive weapon or a bladed article, depending on CLOUGH's intention.

B The knife could be an offensive weapon depending on CLOUGH's intentions, or a bladed article, regardless of his intention.

C The knife would be an offensive weapon or a bladed article, regardless of CLOUGH's intention.

D The knife could be an offensive weapon depending on CLOUGH's intention but it may not be a bladed article, if the length of the blade is under 3.5 inches.

Question 12.7

McGREGOR had been to a traditional Scottish wedding and was wearing the traditional McGregor clan outfit; this included carrying a 'Skean Dhu' knife (with a 3-inch blade) in a sheath in his right sock. Later in the evening, Constable KEEN was on foot patrol in the city centre and saw McGREGOR standing with a group of people in the street outside a pub. The officer saw that McGREGOR was holding the knife and approached to speak to him. McGREGOR stated that he was simply showing the knife to his friends and had no intention of using it to hurt anyone.

Under what circumstances could McGREGOR claim a defence in relation to the knife, under s. 139 of the Criminal Justice Act 1988?

A If he could demonstrate to the court that he had no intention of using the knife to cause injury and it was part of a national costume.

B If he could demonstrate to the court that he had a good reason for having it with him and it was part of a national costume.

C If he could demonstrate to the court that he had it with him as part of a national costume.

D If he could demonstrate to the court that he had no intention of using the knife to cause injury.

Question 12.8

Constable O'NEIL attended a local school providing secondary education in relation to the behaviour of SPEARS, who had been involved in a violent incident. On arrival, the officer discovered that SPEARS, aged 17, had been excluded the year before and had gone to the premises whilst drunk in possession of a knife with a 6-inch blade and had threatened one of the teachers.

Which of the following statements is correct, in relation to an offence under s. 139AA of the Criminal Justice Act 1988?

A This offence is incomplete in these circumstances because SPEARS was not a pupil at the school.

B This offence is complete if it can be shown that SPEARS threatened someone with the knife.

C This offence is complete if it can be shown that SPEARS threatened someone with the knife and there was an immediate risk of serious physical harm to that person.

D This offence is incomplete in these circumstances because a school premises is not a public place.

Question 12.9

CRUZ was employed as a computer software programmer but was sacked for selling material to a rival company. CRUZ returned to the company offices one night, entering the gated compound using an electronic pass that had not been confiscated. CRUZ's intention was to sabotage the company software by loading a virus onto the server. CRUZ was in possession of a knife, intending to use it to threaten the night security guard if necessary. However, CRUZ was unable to get into the main company building as the electronic pass did not work. CRUZ was disturbed by the security guard and ran off.

Has CRUZ committed an offence contrary to s. 8(1) of the Criminal Law Act 1977 (trespassing with a weapon of offence)?

A No, CRUZ has not entered a dwelling with a weapon of offence.

B Yes, CRUZ has entered premises with a weapon of offence.

C No, CRUZ has not entered a building with a weapon of offence.

D No, CRUZ has not entered a dwelling, or land adjacent to a dwelling with a weapon of offence.

Question 12.10

STONE owns a shop which sells second-hand goods and has a reputation for being able to supply unusual weapons. COLLINS entered the shop looking for some weapons for himself and his friends for a football match the following week. STONE indicated that he could get his hands on some knuckle dusters, which he could sell at a good price. COLLINS agreed to return three days later to buy them.

At what point would STONE commit an offence under s. 141 of the Criminal Justice Act 1988?

A Not until he actually sells the weapons to COLLINS.

B Not until he is in possession of the weapons with intent to sell them.

C When he offered to sell the weapons to COLLINS.

D Not until he has the weapons with him with intent to sell them.

Question 12.11

FAHEY is aged 18 and works in a hardware shop. McKAY, aged 17, came into the shop one day and selected a pocket-knife from the display, intending to buy it. The pocket-knife had a blade with a cutting edge of 3.5 inches.

Considering offences under s. 141A of the Criminal Justice Act 1988, could FAHEY lawfully sell this pocket-knife to McKAY?

A Yes, because FAHEY is over 18.

B Yes, because McKAY is over 16.

C No, because McKAY is under 18.

D Yes, this offence does not apply to folding pocket-knives.

Question 12.12

ENLOE (aged 15) is a pupil at St Craymore's School (which is a privately run school offering secondary education to children between the ages of 11 and 16). ENLOE is in the playground of the school when he becomes involved in an argument with INGFIELD who is another pupil at the school. ENLOE produces a knife with a six-inch blade and threatens INGFIELD with it. FROBISHER, a teacher monitoring the playground, sees what has happened and confiscates the knife from ENLOE. INGFIELD is very upset at what has happened and contacts the police via his mobile phone. PC TRINDER is sent to the school and arrives 15 minutes after the call by INGFIELD has been made.

In relation to s. 139B of the Criminal Justice Act 1988 and the power of entry and search associated with it, which of the following comments is right?

A PC TRINDER may enter the school premises and search the premises and any person on the premises if she has reasonable suspicion that an offence under s. 139A of the Criminal Justice Act 1988 (having a bladed or sharply pointed article or offensive weapon on school premises) is being, or has been, committed.

B The power cannot be used in these circumstances as the school is privately run.

C There is a power of entry and search available to the officer but it will not extend to the search of members of staff or employees of the school (such as a search of FROBISHER).

D The threshold for the use of the power under s. 139B is that the officer reasonably believes that an offence under s. 139A (having a bladed or sharply pointed article or offensive weapon on school premises) is being, has been or will be committed. If PC TRINDER has that belief then she may enter the school premises and search the premises and anyone in it for the item concerned.

ANSWERS

Answer 12.1

Answer **C** — Under s. 1(1) of the Prevention of Crime Act 1953, any person who without lawful authority or reasonable excuse, the proof whereof shall lie on him, has with him in any public place any offensive weapon shall be guilty of an offence.

An offence under this section can only be committed in a public place; therefore, answers A, B and D are incorrect.

In relation to the article itself, it has been held that a flick-knife that also operates as a lighter remains an offensive weapon *per se* despite its alternative function (*R v Vasili* [2011] EWCA Crim 615). Therefore, if it *had* been in possession of the person in a public place, answers B and D would have been incorrect for this reason also.

General Police Duties, paras 4.12.2, 4.12.2.5

Answer 12.2

Answer **B** — To prove an offence contrary to s. 1(1) of the Prevention of Crime Act 1953, the prosecution must first show, beyond reasonable doubt, that the defendant had an offensive weapon with him/her. The burden of proof then shifts to the defendant to show that he/she had a 'reasonable excuse' for having the weapon.

There are several overlapping cases that deal with the issue of carrying an offensive weapon, or a bladed or sharply pointed article in a public place in self-defence or to prevent an attack. The common themes with these cases are:

- the defendant's own belief that he/she may be attacked;
- how reasonable that belief was;
- how imminent the attack is likely to be.

The *reasonableness* of the belief was examined in *N v DPP* [2011] EWHC 1807 (Admin). The court found that the defence of reasonable excuse was *not* made out where a person picked up a metal bar for protection having been threatened five minutes earlier by a group of young men in a car who were found to have no weapons. Even if the defendant did believe that he was at risk of an imminent attack, the court held that his belief was not a reasonable one in the circumstances.

Also, it is *not* reasonable to have a weapon with you as a general precaution in case you are attacked (*Evans v Hughes* [1972] 1 WLR 1452) and the court is more likely to uphold an appeal if the fear is reasonable that an attack is imminent, rather than an imprecise attack some time in the future (*R* v *McAuley* [2009] EWCA Crim 2130). Answer D is therefore incorrect.

On the other hand, it *may* be reasonable to have a weapon if you have good grounds to anticipate an unprovoked or unlawful attack, for example for a person guarding cash transits (*Malnik* v *DPP* [1989] Crim LR 451), or if you could show on the balance of probabilities that you were in fear of an imminent attack (see *McAuley* noted previously). This approach was confirmed by the Court of Appeal in *R* v *Emmanuel* [1998] Crim LR 347, where it was accepted that 'good reason' could include self-defence. Answer A is therefore incorrect.

None of these cases suggests that this defence is *only* applicable if you have armed yourself instantaneously, for example immediately prior to an attack, and therefore answer C is incorrect.

General Police Duties, paras 4.12.2.2, 4.12.4.1

Answer 12.3

Answer **A** — The expression 'has with him' will not in most cases include circumstances where a person has an 'innocent' article, which he/she uses offensively. The purpose of the Prevention of Crime Act 1953 is to prevent people from arming themselves for some future event, and the intention of the Act is to deal with preventative issues.

The case of *Ohlson* v *Hylton* [1975] 1 WLR 724 demonstrates this. The defendant had a bag of tools with him in the course of his trade. He produced a hammer from the bag and used it to hit someone. The court held that, as he had formed the intention to use the hammer *after* it came into his possession, the offence was not made out (answers B and C are therefore incorrect). This decision was followed by several other similar cases (*Bates* v *Bulman* [1979] 1 WLR 1190, *R* v *Dayle* [1974] 1 WLR 181 and *R* v *Humphreys* [1977] Crim LR 225).

This is not to say that 'innocent' articles may never become offensive weapons, such as people carrying screwdrivers to defend themselves: it depends on the immediacy of the conversion from one to another, and therefore answer D is incorrect.

General Police Duties, paras 4.12.2.2, 4.12.2.3

Answer 12.4

Answer **D** — It is possible for more than one person to have the same weapon 'with them' (*R* v *Edmonds* [1963] 2 QB 142), and therefore answers A and C are incorrect.

It would be necessary to prove that they knew of the existence of the weapon in the hands of the other.

In this case it was decided that both parties knew of the existence of the weapon and that they knew the other party had it 'with him' at the time of the offence. Answer B is incorrect as the offence is not complete until this is proved.

General Police Duties, para. 4.12.2.3

Answer 12.5

Answer **D** — The prosecution would have to show that the coins have been adapted to cause injury in order to show that they are offensive weapons. However, once the prosecution have proved this, there is no need to show an intention to use them to cause injury (*Davis* v *Alexander* (1970) 54 Cr App R 398).

Answer A is incorrect because the coins have not been 'made' to cause injury; they are not offensive weapons *per se*. However, the fact that they are not offensive weapons *per se* still does not place a burden upon the prosecution to prove intent to use them (*Davis* v *Alexander*), which is why answer C is incorrect.

Answer B is incorrect because it is the adaptation of the article that is relevant, not the intention of the person carrying it (*Bryan* v *Mott* (1976) 62 Cr App R 71).

If PENFOLD were charged under the third leg of the definition, where the weapon is intended to cause injury, the prosecution would have to prove an intention to cause injury by PENFOLD. This would obviously be a harder case to prove than adaptation in these circumstances.

General Police Duties, para. 4.12.2.5

Answer 12.6

Answer **B** — Under s. 1(1) of the Prevention of Crime Act 1953, any person who without lawful authority or reasonable excuse, the proof whereof shall lie on him, has with him in any public place any offensive weapon shall be guilty of an offence.

Under s. 139 of the Criminal Justice Act 1988, a person commits an offence if he/she has a bladed or sharply pointed article in a public place.

Offensive weapons (under s. 1(1)) fall into three categories for the purposes of this offence, namely, articles:

* made for causing injury (offensive weapons *per se*);
* adapted for causing injury; and
* intended by the person who has them, for causing injury.

The knife carried in this scenario would not count as an offensive weapon *per se* (such as a flick knife or gravity knife) as it was not made for causing injury. Neither has it been adapted for causing injury. It is simply a knife that may be used as a tool; therefore, to prosecute the person under this section, you would have to prove that the person who had the knife intended using it for causing injury. Answer C is incorrect, because the person's intention *is* relevant.

Turning to offences under the Criminal Justice Act 1988, a person commits the offence either by carrying a sharply pointed instrument or a bladed instrument. There is no mention of the intent to use the article for any purpose—having it with you is enough. Answer A is therefore incorrect.

There are defences of lawful authority and reasonable excuse (or good reason) for both offences, and folding pocket knives are excluded *unless* the cutting edge of the blade exceeds 3 inches (7.62 cm) and not 3.5. Answer D is therefore incorrect.

General Police Duties, paras 4.12.2.5, 4.12.4

Answer 12.7

Answer **C** — Under s. 139 of the Criminal Justice Act 1988, a person commits an offence if he/she has a bladed or sharply pointed article in a public place.

Section 139 contains two specific defences:

(4) It shall be a defence for a person charged with an offence under this section to prove that he had good reason or lawful authority for having the article with him in a public place.

(5) Without prejudice to the generality of subsection (4) above, it shall be a defence for a person charged with an offence under this section to prove that he had the article with him—

(a) for use at work;

(b) for religious reasons; or

(c) as part of any national costume.

Therefore, under s. 139, the intention of the person is irrelevant when it comes to these specific defences and answers A and D are incorrect.

The general defence under s. 139(4) is available for people who are carrying weapons that are not covered by the defence contained in subsection (5). McGREGOR would only have to demonstrate to the court that he had it with him as part of a national costume and answer B is incorrect.

General Police Duties, para. 4.12.4.1

Answer 12.8

Answer **C** — Under s. 139AA(1) of the Criminal Justice Act 1988, a person is guilty of an offence if that person:

(a) has an article to which this section applies with him or her in a public place or on school premises,
(b) unlawfully and intentionally threatens another person with the article, and
(c) does so in such a way that there is an immediate risk of serious physical harm to that other person.

This offence is similar to that created in s. 1A of the Prevention of Crime Act 1953 and includes threats to those made on school premises or in a public place. Answer D is incorrect.

The fact that the person is not a pupil of the school is irrelevant and answer A is incorrect.

It must be shown that the person threatened someone with an offensive weapon or a sharply pointed article or article having a blade *and* there was an immediate risk of serious physical harm to that person. Answer B is therefore incorrect.

General Police Duties, para. 4.12.5.1

Answer 12.9

Answer **B** — Under s. 8(1) of the Criminal Law Act 1977, a person who is on any premises as a trespasser, after having entered as such, is guilty of an offence if, without lawful authority or reasonable excuse, he/she has with him/her on the premises any weapon of offence.

Under s. 12 of the 1977 Act, 'premises' for this purpose means:

(1) any building; or
(2) any part of a building under separate occupation;
(3) *any land adjacent to and used/intended for use in connection with a building*;
(4) the site comprising any building(s) together with ancillary land;
(5) any fixed structure;
(6) any movable structure, vehicle or vessel designed or adapted for residential purposes.

Any building, or land adjacent to a building (not just a dwelling), is covered by s. 8(1); therefore, CRUZ has committed the offence and for that reason answers A, C and D are incorrect.

General Police Duties, para. 4.12.6

Answer 12.10

Answer **C**— Section 141 of the Criminal Justice Act 1988 makes it an offence to manu-facture, sell, hire, offer for sale or hire, expose, have in possession for the purpose of sale or hire, or lend or give to another person, any weapon listed in the schedule to the Act (knuckle dusters are included).

The offence may be committed by making an offer—the Act makes no mention of being in possession of the article when the offer is made, which is why answer C is correct (this is similar to a case of offering to supply drugs under the Misuse of Drugs Act 1971).

Although offences would be made out in answers A and B, the offence has already been committed.

Answer D would be an incorrect answer in any circumstances, as unlike the original 1953 Act, which requires a person to have the weapon with him, this offence deals with possession for the purpose of sale or hire.

General Police Duties, para. 4.12.7

Answer 12.11

Answer **C** — Under s. 141A of the Criminal Justice Act 1988, it is an offence for any person to sell to a person under 18 a knife, blade, razor blade, axe, or any article which has a blade or sharp point and is made or adapted for causing injury, therefore answer B is incorrect.

The offence does not apply to a razor blade in a cartridge, where not more than 2 mm of the blade is exposed or to a folding pocket-knife with a blade of less than 3 inches. Since the blade in this question was 3.5 inches, it is covered by s. 141A and therefore answer D is incorrect.

The age of the person making the sale is not relevant (which is why answer A is incorrect).

General Police Duties, para. 4.12.8.1

Answer 12.12

Answer **A** — Section 139B of the Criminal Justice Act 1988 states:

(1) A constable may enter school premises and search those premises and any person on those premises for—
 (a) any article to which section 139 of this Act applies, or
 (b) any offensive weapon within the meaning of section 1 of the Prevention of Crime Act 1953,

if he has reasonable grounds for suspecting that an offence under section 139A of this Act is being, or has been, committed.

The threshold for the constable to use his/her power is 'reasonable grounds for *suspecting*', making answer D incorrect.

'School', under s. 4 of the Education Act 1996, means:

(1) …an educational institution which is outside the further education sector and the higher education sector and is an institution for providing—
(a) primary education,
(b) secondary education, or
(c) both primary and secondary education,
whether or not the institution also provides further education.

It does not matter that the school is a private school, making answer B incorrect.

The power of entry and search is to search any person—this would include members of staff and other employees of the school, making answer C incorrect.

General Police Duties, para. 4.12.5.5

13 Protection of People Suffering from Mental Disorders

STUDY PREPARATION

The Mental Health Act 1983 provides for the care and treatment of people suffering from mental disorders and provides powers for enforcing some of its provisions.

If those powers are executed in good faith, the 1983 Act also provides some protection against criminal and civil liability for the police officers and care workers who use them (s. 139).

The 1983 Act is supported by a Code of Practice that sets out guidance for the police and other agencies when dealing with people suffering mental disorders.

QUESTIONS

Question 13.1

Constable MURPHY was called to an incident in the High Street. On arrival, the officer came across ALLINGTON, who was sat in a public fountain. The officer made enquiries with people in a crowd that had gathered and consequently was considering dealing with ALLINGTON under s. 136 of the Mental Health Act 1983.

Considering powers under s. 136 of the Act, which of the following statements is correct?

A Constable MURPHY may arrest ALLINGTON under s. 136, for her own safety.

B Constable MURPHY may remove ALLINGTON under s. 136, for her own interests or for the protection of other persons.

C Constable MURPHY may remove ALLINGTON under s. 136, if she represents a danger to herself.
D Constable MURPHY may remove ALLINGTON under s. 136, if she represents a danger to herself or other members of the public.

Question 13.2

HENDERSON was taken from a busy shopping centre to a hospital by Constable ANDREWS. The officer had removed HENDERSON to the hospital using powers under s. 136 of the Mental Health Act 1983 because of concerns over his mental well-being. The officer had taken HENDERSON there to have him assessed under the Act.

Considering s. 136 of the Mental Health Act 1983, what is the permitted period of detention in relation to HENDERSON?

A A period of 24 hours beginning at the time HENDERSON arrives at the hospital (the place of safety).
B A period of 36 hours beginning at the time HENDERSON arrives at the hospital (the place of safety).
C A period of 48 hours beginning at the time HENDERSON arrives at the hospital (the place of safety).
D A period of 72 hours beginning at the time HENDERSON arrives at the hospital (the place of safety).

Question 13.3

Magistrates have issued a warrant under s. 135(1) of the Mental Health Act 1983 in relation to SHORT, whose family has been concerned that his mental health has deteriorated significantly recently. The warrant authorises SHORT to be removed to a place of safety.

Which of the following statements is correct, in relation to the execution of the warrant issued by the court?

A The warrant must be executed by a constable, who must be accompanied either by a mental health professional or a registered medical practitioner.
B The warrant must be executed either by a mental health professional or a registered medical practitioner, who may ask for a constable to be present if there is reason to believe SHORT may become violent.
C The warrant may be executed either by a constable or a mental health professional, who must be accompanied by a registered medical practitioner.
D The warrant must be executed by a constable, who must be accompanied by an approved mental health professional and by a registered medical practitioner.

ANSWERS

Answer 13.1

Answer **B** — Section 136 of the Mental Health Act 1983 creates a power for police officers to remove such a person under certain conditions. Under s. 136(1), if a person appears to a constable to be suffering from mental disorder and to be in immediate need of care or control, the constable may, if he thinks it necessary to do so *in the interests of that person or for the protection of other persons*, remove that person to a place of safety.

Section 136 does not mention danger—this power is more to do with caring for individuals and removing them to a place where they can receive appropriate treatment. Answers C and D are therefore incorrect.

Further, there is no power of arrest under s. 136—the person is not being dealt with for an offence, rather, they are being removed to the most appropriate location to deal with their illness. Answer A is therefore incorrect.

General Police Duties, para. 4.13.2

Answer 13.2

Answer **A** — Where a person has been removed to a place of safety by a constable, under s. 136 of the Mental Health Act 1983, he or she may be detained there for a permitted period of detention. The 'permitted period of detention' means the period of *24 hours* beginning at the time when the person arrives at the hospital (the place of safety (s. 136(2A)(a)(i)).

Answers B, C and D are therefore incorrect.

General Police Duties, para. 4.13.2

Answer 13.3

Answer **D** — Under s. 135(1) of the Mental Health Act 1983, where there is reasonable cause to suspect that a person believed to be suffering from a mental disorder:

(a) has been, or is being ill-treated or neglected, or
(b) is unable to care for himself/herself and is living alone,

a warrant may be issued by a magistrate authorising a *constable* to enter any premises specified and to remove the person to a place of safety.

Answers B and C are therefore incorrect.

In doing so, the officer *must* be accompanied by an approved mental health professional and by a registered medical practitioner. Answer A is therefore incorrect.

General Police Duties, para. 4.13.3

14 | Offences Relating to Land and Premises

STUDY PREPARATION

The Criminal Justice and Public Order Act 1994 allows the criminal courts to deal with offences of trespass. This chapter deals with offences such as trespassing with intent to disrupt lawful activities, trespassing with intent to reside on land and residing in vehicles on land.

Do not ignore the offences of being found on enclosed premises and causing a nuisance on educational premises; both are useful offences to remember.

QUESTIONS

Question 14.1

A new football stadium is being built on the outskirts of a town. Vehicles belonging to the building company have been parked in an enclosed warehouse situated adjacent to the building site, which is due to be demolished after the stadium is completed. Environmental protestors have been attempting to stop the building work. The builders arrived for work one morning and as they opened the doors to the warehouse, a number of protestors stormed in and chained themselves to the vehicles, intending to disrupt the building work. Building work was disrupted for several hours as the police were called to remove them. It was a peaceful protest; no property was damaged and no one was threatened.

Have the protesters committed an offence under s. 68 of the Criminal Justice and Public Order Act 1994 (aggravated trespass), in these circumstances?

A No, as the protestors were not on land in the open air.

B Yes, the offence is complete in these circumstances.

C No, as the protestors were not on land where the building work was due to take place.

D No, as the protestors did not threaten or intimidate the builders, or cause damage.

Question 14.2

OSMAND and WREN entered a building site as trespassers; they were protesting against the construction of a new shopping centre. They had with them a large concrete tube, which they placed on the ground in the middle of the site. OSMAND and WREN then connected their arms through the tube with a padlocked chain. Inspector CARTER was the senior officer to arrive and concluded that they had committed an offence contrary to s. 68 of the Criminal Justice and Public Order Act 1994 (aggravated trespass) and directed them to leave. OSMAND and WREN stated that they were unable to leave because they had no key to the padlock. Eventually a locksmith was called to the scene and when they were released, OSMAND and WREN were arrested for failing to leave when directed, under s. 69 of the Act. They were charged with the offence under s. 69 and later in court, claimed they had a reasonable excuse for failing to leave as soon as practicable—that they were unable to do so until they were released.

Could OSMAND and WREN's defence succeed in these circumstances?

A No, they did not leave the site as soon as practicable.

B Yes, they left the site as soon as practicable after they were released.

C No, their intention was to frustrate the police utilising their powers under this Act and they succeeded.

D No, their intention when they chained themselves to the tube is irrelevant; they succeeded in disrupting lawful activities on the site.

Question 14.3

The police attended an alarm at an office building in a city centre. They made a search of the premises and found PECK, who was hiding in one of the offices. The officers recognised PECK as a homeless person with whom police regularly had dealings. Following questioning during which it was established that PECK was merely looking for shelter, the officers decided that there was insufficient evidence to arrest PECK for burglary.

Would the premises that PECK was found on amount to an 'inclosed premises', for the purposes of offences under s. 4 of the Vagrancy Act 1824?

A No, 'inclosed premises' will only include outhouses and land ancillary to buildings.

B No, if the person is found in a building, that building must be a dwelling for the purposes of this offence.

C Yes, provided the person is found in a building, or outhouse or land ancillary to a building; it doesn't matter what type of building.

D No, a room within an office building will not amount to an enclosed area for the purposes of this offence.

Question 14.4

Constable PARRY was called to a high school at 4 pm on a Saturday by the caretaker, POINTER. It would appear that teenagers, who attended the school, were entering the playing fields on weekends and using them as a meeting area. POINTER stated that the teenagers were generally well-behaved, but their presence caused him nuisance as he had to work extra hours on weekends, to make sure they did not cause a disturbance.

Considering s. 547(1) of the Education Act 1996, have the children committed an offence in this situation?

A No, there is no evidence that the children are causing a disturbance.

B No, the children are gathering when the school is closed; therefore, they are not causing a nuisance to anyone.

C Yes, they could be causing a nuisance or disturbance to the annoyance of POINTER, who lawfully uses the premises.

D No, even though they may be causing a nuisance or disturbance to the annoyance of POINTER, they are not interrupting lessons at the school.

Question 14.5

John and Lesley NESBITT (husband and wife) wish to protest against the building of several new houses on private land near to their home. They make several signs illustrating their opposition to the construction and enter a field next to the construction site. The field is common land. They shout at workers on the building site intending to disrupt their building work. PC VOLT (an officer in uniform) is sent to the incident. The NESBITTs are extremely polite to the officer but tell him in no uncertain terms that they are doing nothing wrong and that there is nothing he can do to stop them exercising their lawful rights.

Would PC VOLT be able to remove John and Lesley NESBITT from the common land using the power under s. 69 of the Criminal Justice and Public Order Act 1994 (power to remove persons)?

A No, the power to remove John and Lesley NESBITT would not be available to PC VOLT as it must be authorised by an officer of at least the rank of inspector.

B Yes, if PC VOLT reasonably believes that John and Lesley NESBITT intend to trespass on the building site (private land) and disrupt the lawful activity that is taking place there.

C No, the power is not available to PC VOLT as John and Lesley NESBITT are not committing the offence of aggravated trespass (under s. 68 of the Act) nor are they simply trespassing on land.

D Yes, if PC VOLT reasonably suspects that John and Lesley NESBITT intend to trespass on the building site (private land) and disrupt the lawful activity that is taking place there.

ANSWERS

Answer 14.1

Answer **B** — Under s. 68(1) of the Criminal Justice and Public Order Act 1994, a person commits the offence of aggravated trespass if he/she trespasses on land and, in relation to any lawful activity which persons are engaging in or are about to engage in on that or adjoining land, does there anything which is intended by him/her to have the effect:

- (a) of intimidating those persons or any of them so as to deter them or any of them from engaging in that activity,
- (b) of obstructing that activity, or
- (c) of disrupting that activity.

Therefore, even though the protestors did not threaten or intimidate the builders, or cause damage, their actions were sufficient to obstruct and disrupt the activity. Answer D is therefore incorrect.

The offence is committed when a person trespasses on land where the activity is due to take place or on *adjoining* land (which makes answer C incorrect).

Section 68 originally included the phrase 'in the open air' but it was removed by the Anti-social Behaviour Act 2003. In *DPP* v *Chivers* [2010] EWHC 1814 (Admin), it was held that the purpose and effect of this amendment was quite plainly to include buildings. This situation remains the same and answer A is incorrect.

Note that in order to establish the offence of aggravated trespass under s. 68, you must prove that the defendant had committed the act(s) complained of in the physical presence of a person engaged or about to engage in the lawful activity with which the defendant wished to interfere (*DPP* v *Tilly* [2001] EWHC 821 (Admin)).

General Police Duties, para. 4.14.2

Answer 14.2

Answer **B** — Section 68(1) of the Criminal Justice and Public Order Act 1994 states that a person commits the offence of aggravated trespass if he trespasses on land and, in relation to any lawful activity which persons are engaging in or are about to engage in on that or adjoining land, does there anything which is intended by him/her to have the effect:

(a) of intimidating those persons or any of them so as to deter them or any of them from engaging in that activity,

(b) of obstructing that activity, or

(c) of disrupting that activity.

The intent of the defendant *is* relevant—if they have not committed the offence of aggravated trespass, then the order under s. 69 directing them to leave is invalid; answer D is therefore incorrect.

It is a defence for the accused to show that they were not trespassing on the land, or had a reasonable excuse for failing to leave the land as soon as practicable or for again entering the land as a trespasser (s. 69(4)).

In circumstances similar to this question, the court quashed the appellants' convictions for failing to leave a shop premises as soon as practicable when so directed by the police, because they were physically unable to move until they had been unchained, and had left as soon as this was done. Answer A is therefore incorrect.

The court also held that what they did was designed to disrupt the shop's trade, not to frustrate the operation of s. 69; the fact that they had voluntarily (and deliberately) placed themselves in a situation in which they could not leave when directed was held to be irrelevant (*Nero* v *DPP* [2012] EWHC 1238 (Admin) and *Richardson* v *Director of Public Prosecutions* [2014] UKSC 8). Answer C is therefore incorrect.

General Police Duties, paras 4.14.2 to 4.14.2.2

Answer 14.3

Answer **D** — It is a summary offence under s. 4(1) of the Vagrancy Act 1824 for any person to be found in or upon any dwelling house, warehouse, coach house, stable or outhouse or in any enclosed yard, garden or area for *any unlawful purpose*. This offence was created to prevent vagrancy and the definition gives a clue as to the type of premises that might be considered inclosed:

(i) every person being found in or upon any dwelling house, warehouse, coach-house, stable, or outhouse, or in any inclosed yard, garden, or area, for any unlawful purpose; commits an offence.

Answers A and B are incorrect as the Act covers many buildings that are not merely dwellings or outhouses and land ancillary to buildings.

However, a room within an office building has been held *not* to amount to an enclosed area for the purposes of this offence (*Talbot* v *Oxford City Justices* [2000] 1 WLR 1102). Answer C is therefore incorrect.

General Police Duties, para. 4.14.6

Answer 14.4

Answer **C** — Under s. 547(1) of the Education Act 1996:

> Any person who without lawful authority is present on premises to which this section applies and causes or permits nuisance or disturbance to the annoyance of persons who lawfully use those premises (whether or not any such persons are present at the time) [shall be guilty of an offence].

This offence is designed to deal with nuisance such as disturbing lessons or other school-related activities; however, the offence may still be committed when the people who usually use the school (pupils and teachers) are not present. Answers B and D are therefore incorrect.

The offence may be committed by causing a nuisance *or* a disturbance to the annoyance of persons who lawfully use those premises. A caretaker would qualify as such a person and while the children may not have been causing a disturbance, they were most certainly causing a nuisance. Answer A is therefore incorrect.

General Police Duties, para. 4.14.7

Answer 14.5

Answer **C** — Section 69 of the Criminal Justice and Public Order Act 1994 states:

> (1) If the senior police officer present at the scene reasonably believes—
>   (a) that a person is committing, has committed or intends to commit the offence of aggravated trespass on land; or
>   (b) that two or more persons are trespassing on land and are present there with the common purpose of intimidating persons so as to deter them from engaging in a lawful activity or of obstructing or disrupting a lawful activity,
> he may direct that person or (as the case may be) those persons (or any of them) to leave the land.

The power under s. 69 can be authorised by the senior officer present (making answer A incorrect). The power is only available in the above circumstances and as John and Lesley NESBITT are doing nothing wrong (they have not committed the offence of aggravated trespass nor are they trespassing on land) the power is not available no matter what PC VOLT suspects or believes, making answer C correct and answers B and D incorrect.

General Police Duties, paras 4.14.2, 4.14.2.1

15 Licensing and Offences Relating to Alcohol

STUDY PREPARATION

The Licensing Act 2003 places emphasis firmly on the holders of personal licences to run orderly premises, taking into account such matters as crime and disorder, public safety and protection of children. You should also learn the powers to enter premises and, once inside, how to deal with offences and/or drunkenness.

Further powers of enforcement are provided, allowing the courts to make an order requiring licensed premises to be closed.

QUESTIONS

Question 15.1

CALE is the chair of a residents' association on a housing estate. The Anchor public house on the estate has caused considerable concern recently due to the number of public order incidents that have occurred in the vicinity of the premises on weekends. CALE and other residents have raised the issue several times in meetings with local police groups as their perception is that the police and the local authority are reluctant to take action against the licensee.

In which circumstances could a review of the premises licence take place?

A A review of a licence may take place if the licensee is failing to take sufficient measures to prevent public nuisance, or where the police consider that measures put in place to prevent crime and disorder are not being effective.

B A review of a licence may take place if the licensee is failing to take sufficient measures to prevent crime and disorder.

C A review of a licence may take place if the licensee is failing to take sufficient measures to prevent public nuisance or crime and disorder.

D A review of a licence may take place if the licensee is failing to take sufficient measures to prevent public nuisance.

Question 15.2

Section 97 of the Licensing Act 2003 provides a power of entry for a constable to enter and search any premises which hold a club premises certificate.

What restrictions are placed on this power of entry and search?

A Entry is allowed to detect licensing offences or to prevent a breach of the peace only.

B Entry is allowed to prevent a breach of the peace only.

C Entry is allowed to detect licensing offences, to search for offences relating to the supply of drugs, or to prevent a breach of the peace.

D Entry is allowed to search for offences relating to the supply of drugs, or to prevent a breach of the peace only.

Question 15.3

Constable KHAN was on duty as part of a plain-clothes team of police officers, working with LEWIS, a licensing officer from the local authority and a person authorised under the Licensing Act 2003. The team was tasked with visiting public houses in the locality to identify licensing offences. They arrived at the Royal Oak public house at 10.50 pm and identified themselves (as a police officer and licensing officer) to GEORGE, the door supervisor, and asked to enter the premises. GEORGE refused, stating the premises were about to close. The operating schedule stated that the premises should close at 11 pm.

Does either Constable KHAN or LEWIS have the power to enter the premises using reasonable force under the Licensing Act 2003?

A No, the power to enter by reasonable force is restricted to uniformed officers only.

B Constable KHAN only; LEWIS does not have a power to enter by force in these circumstances.

C Yes, both have the power to enter using reasonable force in these circumstances.

D Yes, but only if they have reason to believe that offences are being committed.

Question 15.4

The police have been called to a call centre where NUGENT works. When the officers arrived they entered a private part of the building where entry was restricted to employees of the company. They were told by NUGENT's manager that she had returned to the office at lunchtime and was drunk. She had started an argument with her line manager and when they approached her they could see she was clearly drunk and acting in a disorderly manner.

Assuming that the necessity test is applicable, could the officers arrest NUGENT for an offence of being drunk and disorderly, under s. 91(1) of the Criminal Justice Act 1967?

A No, the offence must be committed in a public place.
B Yes, the offence may be committed anywhere.
C No, the offence may not be committed inside a building.
D Yes, because NUGENT was not inside a dwelling at the time.

Question 15.5

Constable MURRAY was called to an incident in the Dog public house. The licensee led the officer to the toilet area where they saw LEWIS who was slumped in a corner in a drunken condition, covered in vomit. The officer tried to wake LEWIS, but was unable to do so as he was so drunk. The officer was considering arresting LEWIS for being found drunk.

Assuming that the necessity test is applicable, does Constable MURRAY have the power to deal with LEWIS under s. 12 of the Licensing Act 1872 (being found drunk)?

A No, the offence must be committed in a public place.
B Yes, the offence may be committed anywhere.
C No, the offence may not be committed in a building.
D Yes, the offence may be committed on licensed premises.

Question 15.6

GREEN owns an off-licence which is being monitored by the local Neighbourhood Policing Team, because of complaints that alcohol is being sold to young people on a regular basis. During an operation in March, the police caught GREEN selling alcohol to ZENDEN, aged 16. In April, the police again detected GREEN selling alcohol to ZENDEN on one other occasion.

Would GREEN's behaviour amount to an offence under s. 147A of the Licensing Act 2003 (persistently selling alcohol to children under the age of 18)?

A Yes, GREEN has sold alcohol to a person under 18, on two or more occasions, within a period of three consecutive months.

B No, GREEN has not sold alcohol to a person under 18, on three or more occasions, in three consecutive months.

C Yes, and this is a 'strict liability' offence so GREEN would not have any defence available in answer to a charge under s. 147A of the Act.

D No, GREEN has not sold alcohol to a person under 18, on four or more occasions, in three consecutive months.

Question 15.7

Whilst on patrol in a park in the evening, Constable MANNING saw a group of four young people, all drinking from bottles of beer. The officer discovered that three of the group were 17 years of age and the youngest, GRANT, was under 15. Constable MANNING confiscated the alcohol from the group and disposed of it.

What does s. 1 of the Confiscation of Alcohol (Young Persons) Act 1997 state about the actions Constable MANNING should now take?

A Constable MANNING may take names and addresses from all of the group and may remove GRANT to his place of residence or a place of safety.

B Constable MANNING must take names and addresses from all of the group and must remove GRANT to his place of residence or a place of safety.

C Constable MANNING shall require all the persons in the group to state their names and addresses and may remove GRANT to his place of residence or a place of safety.

D Constable MANNING must take names and addresses from all of the group and may remove everyone in the group to their place of residence or a place of safety.

Question 15.8

Constable SINGH was walking through a park when he came across two young people, who were intoxicated. He discovered they were 15 years old and that they had been given drink by HAWKINS. Constable SINGH intercepted HAWKINS, who was walking away from the park, and saw that he was in possession of a can of lager from which he was drinking. HAWKINS is over 18 years old.

What are Constable SINGH's powers to deal with HAWKINS in these circumstances?

A He has the power to confiscate the alcohol from HAWKINS and demand his name and address.

B He has no powers, as HAWKINS did not intend to supply the alcohol to a person under 18.

C He has no powers, as HAWKINS is not under 18.

D He has no powers, as HAWKINS is not in the company of a person under 18 to whom he intends to supply the alcohol.

Question 15.9

The police have conducted a series of test purchase operations over a period of a month at the Cherry Tree public house, due to suspected under-age drinking. The officers conducting the exercise have reported that GREEN, the premises licence holder, served alcohol to five under-age drinkers during this period. The duty inspector considers that an offence has been committed under s. 147A of the Licensing Act 2003, and a closure notice should be served on GREEN, to prevent further sales to young people.

Which of the following statements is correct, in relation to such a notice, under s. 169A of the Act?

A The inspector may authorise a closure notice, provided GREEN accepts responsibility for the offence under s. 147A.

B The inspector may authorise a closure notice in these circumstances alone.

C A superintendent may authorise a closure, provided GREEN accepts responsibility for the offence under s. 147A.

D A superintendent may authorise a closure, provided there is a realistic prospect of prosecuting GREEN for an offence under s. 147A.

Question 15.10

Staff from a Neighbourhood Policing Team have been meeting with partners from the local authority to discuss problems relating to ongoing serious anti-social behaviour on a housing estate. Consideration is being given to making a Public Spaces Protection Order to assist the partners in dealing with the problem.

Which of the following statements is correct, in relation to making such an order, under s. 59 of the Anti-social Behaviour, Crime and Policing Act 2014?

A The order may be made either by a superintendent or an equivalent person in the local authority, provided it can be demonstrated that they have consulted with each other.

B The order must be made and publicised by the local authority, in consultation with the chief officer of police, the Police and Crime Commissioner and any representatives of the local community they consider appropriate.

C The order may be made either by a superintendent or an equivalent person in the local authority, provided it can be demonstrated that they have consulted with each other and publicised the details of the order locally.

D The order may be made either by an inspector or an equivalent person in the local authority, in consultation with any representatives of the local community they consider appropriate.

Question 15.11

Local licensing officers working in partnership have met urgently on a Saturday morning to discuss the Carpenters Arms public house, which has been the location of serious disorder over the last three weekends. A closure notice had been issued to the licence holder the previous evening following a fight between two rival gangs at the premises. The officers were preparing a file to take to court to apply for a closure order to prevent the premises opening again that night, because intelligence had shown that further violence was likely to occur.

Which of the following statements is correct, in relation to an application for a closure order, under s. 160 of the Licensing Act 2003?

A The application may be made by an inspector or an equivalent person from the local authority.

B The application may be made by a superintendent or an equivalent person from the local authority.

C The application may only be made by a superintendent.

D The application may only be made by a member of the licensing authority for the area.

Question 15.12

A closure order has been made in respect of the Heathcock public house, which has been the location of serious disorder over the weekend. The request was made for the order to allow the local licensing authority to meet urgently to discuss the problems at the premises and any potential solutions.

If the order was granted, how long would it last, according to s. 160 of the Licensing Act 2003?

A The premises could be closed for a period not exceeding 24 hours.

B The premises could be closed for a period not exceeding 48 hours.

C The premises could be closed for a period not exceeding 7 days.

D The premises could be closed for a period not exceeding 14 days.

Question 15.13

Constable WARREN works as a Licensing Officer based in a co-located office with the local authority Licensing Department. Constable WARREN has attended premises in High Street with CANTEBURY, a local authority Licensing Officer. They have received intelligence that NEWMAN is using the premises for the unlicensed sale of alcohol. Their intention is to gather evidence and, if necessary, close the premises down.

Section 19 of the Criminal Justice and Police Act 2001 allows for a closure notice to be served in respect of unlicensed premises. In respect of this power, which of the following statements is correct?

A A closure notice may be served by Constable WARREN only, provided this is done in consultation with the local authority (which would include consulting with CANTEBURY).

B Either Constable WARREN or CANTEBURY could serve a closure notice in these circumstances.

C A closure notice may only be served by an inspector; neither Constable WARREN nor CANTEBURY has the authority to do so in these circumstances.

D A closure notice may only be authorised by a magistrate; either Constable WARREN or CANTEBURY would have to apply to the court for such a notice.

ANSWERS

Answer 15.1

Answer **A** — A premises licence may be reviewed by a licensing authority where it is considered a licensee is failing to take sufficient measures to prevent public nuisance, or where the police consider that measures put in place to prevent crime and disorder are not being effective.

Answers B, C and D are therefore incorrect.

General Police Duties, para. 4.15.4.1

Answer 15.2

Answer **D** — Under s. 97 of the Licensing Act 2003, where a club premises certificate has effect in respect of any premises, a constable may enter and search the premises if he/she has reasonable cause to believe:

(a) that an offence under section 4(3)(a), (b) or (c) of the Misuse of Drugs Act 1971 (supply-ing or offering to supply, or being concerned in supplying or making an offer to supply, a controlled drug) has been, is being, or is about to be, committed there, or

(b) that there is likely to be a breach of the peace there.

This section does not allow a constable to enter the premises to detect licensing offences; therefore, answers A and C are incorrect. Entry is allowed (using reasonable force if necessary) in order to detect offences under the Misuse of Drugs Act 1971, or if a breach of the peace is likely to occur in the premises. Answers A and B are incorrect for this reason.

General Police Duties, para. 4.15.4.3

Answer 15.3

Answer **C** — Under s. 179 of the Licensing Act 2003, where a constable or an author-ised person has reason to believe that any premises are being, or are about to be, used for a licensable activity, they may enter the premises with a view to seeing whether the activity is being, or is to be, carried on under and in accordance with an authorisa-tion (s. 179(1)). A person exercising the power conferred by this section may, if neces-sary, use reasonable force (s. 179(3)). Since the power under this section is not restricted to police officers, answer B is incorrect. Also, there is no requirement for a police officer to be in uniform; therefore, answer A is incorrect.

There is a separate power, under s. 180 of the Act, for a constable to enter premises in order to investigate offences. A constable may enter by reasonable force under this section. However, s. 179 shows that a constable or authorised person may enter premises using reasonable force simply to make sure that licensing activities are being carried out within the law. Answer D is therefore incorrect.

(Note that an authorised person exercising the powers conferred on them must, if so requested, produce evidence of their authority to exercise the power.)

General Police Duties, paras 4.15.5

Answer 15.4

Answer **A** — Under s. 91(1) of the Criminal Justice Act 1967, a person commits an offence if, in a public place, he/she is guilty, while drunk, of disorderly conduct. Since the offence may only be committed in a public place, answers B, C and D are incorrect.

General Police Duties, para. 4.15.8

Answer 15.5

Answer **D** — Under s. 12 of the Licensing Act 1902, every person found drunk in any highway or other public place, whether a building or not, or on any licensed premises, shall be liable.

The offence may not be committed 'anywhere', but may be committed inside a building or in a licensed premises. Answers B and C are therefore incorrect.

Similarly, the offence is not restricted to public places only; for example, a licensed premises which is closed may not be a public place; however, a person may be found drunk on the premises after everyone else has left and the offence may be committed in those circumstances. Answer A is therefore incorrect.

General Police Duties, para. 4.15.9

Answer 15.6

Answer **A** — Under s. 147A(1) of the Licensing Act 2003, a person is guilty of an offence if:

(a) on 2 or more different occasions within a period of 3 consecutive months alcohol is unlawfully sold on the same premises to an individual aged under 18.

It is 'unlawfully sold' if the person making the sale believed the individual to be under 18 or did not have reasonable grounds for believing them to be 18 or over (a defence to the offence, making answer C incorrect).

The offence is committed if alcohol is sold on 'two or more different occasions'. Answers B and D are therefore incorrect.

General Police Duties, para. 4.15.10

Answer 15.7

Answer **C** — Under s. 1 of the Confiscation of Alcohol (Young Persons) Act 1997, apart from the power to confiscate any alcohol from young people under the age of 18 under subss. (1) and (2) in certain conditions (which applied in this case), a constable has further duties and powers, as follows:

(1AA) A constable who imposes a requirement on a person under subsection (1) shall also require the person to state the person's name and address.
(1AB) A constable who imposes a requirement on a person under subsection (1) may, if the constable reasonably suspects that the person is under the age of 16, remove the person to the person's place of residence or a place of safety.

The duty to ask for the person's name and address under s. 1(1AA) is not just a power, it is a requirement and answer A is incorrect.

On the other hand, the constable is not *required* to remove a person under 16 to their place of residence or a place of safety and this power is not available to the rest of the people in the group, who were over 16. Answers B and D are therefore incorrect.

General Police Duties, para. 4.15.11.2

Answer 15.8

Answer **A** — Under s. 1(1) of the Confiscation of Alcohol (Young Persons) Act 1997, a constable who reasonably suspects that a person who is in a relevant place is in possession of alcohol, may confiscate the alcohol if:

(a) the person is under 18; *or*
(b) the person intends that any of the alcohol shall be consumed by a person under 18 in a relevant place; *or*
(c) the person is with *or* has recently been with a person under 18 and that person has recently consumed alcohol in the relevant place.

Under s. 1(6), a 'relevant place' is:

- any public place, other than licensed premises; or
- any place, other than a public place, to which that person has unlawfully gained access;

and for this purpose a place is a public place if, at the material time, the public or any section of the public has access to it—on payment or otherwise—as of right or by virtue of express or implied permission.

Under para. (c), as HAWKINS has recently been with a person under 18 who has consumed alcohol, regardless of whether he intends to supply more alcohol to the children, the officer will have the power to confiscate the alcohol he is in possession of. Answers B and D are therefore incorrect.

Also, alcohol may be confiscated from a person who is over 18 if he/she has committed an act mentioned under paras (b) and (c)—the power is designed to prevent alcohol either being consumed by, or supplied to, people under 18. Answer C is therefore incorrect.

Note that subs. (1AA) of the Act states that a constable exercising the power under s. 1 *shall* require the person to state their name and address.

General Police Duties, para. 4.15.11.2

Answer 15.9

Answer **D** — Section 169A of the Licensing Act 2003 provides that a senior police officer (of the rank of superintendent or higher), or an inspector of weights and measures, may give a closure notice where there is evidence that a person has committed the offence of persistently selling alcohol to children at the premises in question. Answers A and B are therefore incorrect.

A further condition exists under s. 169A—the superintendent must consider that the evidence is such that there would be a realistic prospect of conviction if the offender was prosecuted for it. Answer C is therefore incorrect.

General Police Duties, para. 4.15.11.4

Answer 15.10

Answer **B** — Under s. 59 of the Anti-social Behaviour, Crime and Policing Act 2014, a local authority may make a Public Spaces Protection Order if satisfied on reasonable grounds that activities carried on in a public place within the authority's area have had, or are likely to have, a detrimental effect on the quality of life of those in the locality.

The power to make the order lies with the local authority. Answers A, C and D are therefore incorrect.

General Police Duties, para. 4.15.12.1

Answer 15.11

Answer **C** — Under s. 160(1) of the Licensing Act 2003, where there is or is expected to be disorder in any local justice area, a magistrates' court acting in the area may make an order requiring all premises which are situated at or near the place of the disorder or expected disorder, and in respect of which a premises licence or a temporary event notice has effect, to be closed for a period, not exceeding 24 hours, specified in the order.

A magistrates' court may make an order under this section only on the application of a police officer who is of the rank of superintendent or above (s. 160(2)).

Answers A, B and D are therefore incorrect.

General Police Duties, para. 4.15.13

Answer 15.12

Answer **A** — Under s. 160(1) of the Licensing Act 2003, where there is or is expected to be disorder in any local justice area, a magistrates' court acting in the area may make an order requiring all premises which are situated at or near the place of the disorder or expected disorder, and in respect of which a premises licence or a temporary event notice has effect, to be closed for a period, not exceeding 24 hours, specified in the order.

Answers B, C and D are therefore incorrect.

General Police Duties, para. 4.15.13

Answer 15.13

Answer **B** — Under s. 19 of the Criminal Justice and Police Act 2001, where a constable is satisfied that any premises (including land or any place whether covered or not):

- are being used or
- have been used within the last 24 hours
- for the unlicensed sale/exposure for sale
- of alcohol
- for consumption on or in the vicinity of the premises

he/she may serve a closure notice.

This power is available to any police officer of any rank; therefore, Constable WARREN does not need to call an inspector or go to court. Answers C and D are therefore incorrect.

In addition, under s. 19, the power to serve a notice is available to any police officer of any rank and *may also be exercised by the relevant local authority*. Answer A is therefore incorrect.

General Police Duties, para. 4.15.14

16 | Offences and Powers Relating to Information

STUDY PREPARATION

The management of information is an area of importance to the police generally and therefore to its supervisors, managers, trainers and examiners.

The key issues here are the statutory restrictions on who can access what type of information and for what purpose. Much accessing of information involves the use of computers and it is therefore necessary to understand the relevant aspects of the Computer Misuse Act 1990.

A significant part of this chapter contains the provisions of the Regulation of Investigatory Powers Act 2000 (RIPA), which covers the covert acquisition of information about people, through the use of covert human intelligence sources (CHIS), surveillance and the interception of communications.

QUESTIONS

Question 16.1

MORTON is a well-known public figure and is taking legal advice about bringing a case against the police, under Art. 8 of the European Convention on Human Rights (respect for private and family life). The circumstances were that MORTON reported to the police her suspicion that someone was trying to hack into her emails. MORTON alleges that the police failed to act and as a result, the hacker subsequently managed to download several photographs of her with no clothes on, from emails sent by a friend. The photographs were displayed on the Internet and MORTON claims this was potentially ruinous to her career.

Which of the following statements is correct, in relation to MORTON's potential claim?

A The aim of Art. 8 is to protect a person's life from interference by 'public authorities': it therefore does not apply in these circumstances.

B The State has a positive obligation to prevent others from interfering with an individual's right to private and family life; therefore, Art. 8 may apply in these circumstances.

C The State has a positive obligation to prevent others from interfering with an individual's right to private and family life, but this does not extend to a person's correspondence; therefore, Art. 8 would not apply in these circumstances.

D The State has a positive obligation to prevent others from interfering with an individual's right to private and family life, but this duty only extends to maintaining public safety; therefore, Art. 8 would not apply in these circumstances.

Question 16.2

Section 1 of the Computer Misuse Act 1990 makes provision in relation to unauthorised access to computer material.

Where a person is not authorised and they have the required intent and knowledge, at which point would an offence under this section first be committed?

A When the computer is switched on.
B When the 'log on screen' is filled out.
C When they are successfully logged onto the system.
D When the actual program is accessed.

Question 16.3

BIGNELL worked for a large bank and was dating BRADY who, unknown to her, had ties with an organised crime gang. BRADY persuaded BIGNELL to access information from customers' accounts and pass the details to him. BIGNELL is not authorised to access the information, but does as BRADY asks. BRADY was actually selling on the data to credit card forgers—a fact that BIGNELL was unaware of.

What would have to be proved, in order to convict BIGNELL of an offence contrary to s. 1 of the Computer Misuse Act 1990?

A That she was not authorised to access the data and that she knew this was the case.

B That she was not authorised to access the data and that she knew this was the case, or was reckless as to whether or not this was the case.

C Only that she was not authorised to access the data.

D That she was not authorised to access the data and that she knew what the information was being used for.

Question 16.4

LENNON was a computer software engineer who worked for a company which distributed electronic equipment bought by customers online. LENNON was sacked by the company for allegedly stealing. Seeking revenge, LENNON devised a program which sent three million emails to the company's inbox in one day. LENNON hoped that the volume of emails would cause the company's online computer package to crash. However, another software engineer working for the company realised what was happening and implemented a program which intercepted the emails. In the end, no damage was done to the company.

If LENNON were to be prosecuted for an offence under s. 3 of the Computer Misuse Act 1990, which of the following statements would be correct in respect of the 'intent' required for this offence?

A The prosecution would have to show that LENNON intended causing an economic loss to the company.

B The prosecution must show that LENNON intended to impair the operation of the company's software program.

C The prosecution would have to show that LENNON intended to impair the operation of the company's software program, or was reckless as to whether it would be impaired.

D The prosecution would have to show that LENNON intended causing permanent damage to the company's computer program.

Question 16.5

Constable PETERS is a member of a Neighbourhood Policing Team on a housing estate which suffers from a significant drug problem. The officer has formed a good relationship with young people in the area and has been approached by GAMLIN who lives on the estate and is aged 14. GAMLIN has disclosed to the officer that her older brother (who is 23 years old), whom she lives with, but does not get on with, is actively dealing heroin. She told Constable PETERS that she would like to give regular information about her brother's activities. The officer has returned to the station and has sought advice from the specialists in this area of policing.

In these circumstances, could officers seek authority to recruit GAMLIN as a CHIS?

A No, on no occasion should the use or conduct of a CHIS be authorised when he/she is under 16 years of age.

B Yes, subject to the special provisions that apply to all juvenile CHISs.

C No, on no occasion should the use or conduct of a CHIS under 16 years of age be authorised to give information against someone in the same household as the person.

D No, on no occasion should the use or conduct of a CHIS under 16 years of age be authorised to give information against someone in the same family as the person.

Question 16.6

Detective Inspector GREEN has been telephoned by DC CALDWELL, an officer working in the Drug Squad. The officer has received information that a large quantity of drugs is due to be moved into the area within the next hour to an address well known to the team. DC CALDWELL is at court applying for a warrant to search the premises, but wishes to set up a directed surveillance operation urgently to monitor the address.

Is Detective Inspector GREEN able to give an urgent authority for directed surveillance?

A No, inspectors are only able to give urgent authorities for CHIS activity.

B Yes, Detective Inspector GREEN may give an urgent authority if it is not reasonably practicable to have the application considered by a superintendent.

C Yes, inspectors are able to give authorities for directed surveillance in any situation; the restrictions relating to urgent authorities apply to CHIS activity.

D No, only a superintendent is able to give urgent authorities.

Question 16.7

Superintendent MILLER has given an urgent authorisation for CHIS activity by GOUGH, who has passed on information to the police about a potential bomb-making 'factory' in a house in the neighbourhood. GOUGH has been tasked, within strict parameters, to find out more information while the police organise an armed response.

Given that the CHIS has been authorised orally, which of the following statements is correct as to how long the authorisation should last?

A The authorisation will last for 24 hours unless renewed.

B The authorisation will last for 48 hours unless renewed.

C The authorisation will last for 72 hours unless renewed.

D Because it has been given by a superintendent, is will last for 12 months.

Question 16.8

DAWSON was arrested for a series of frauds against elderly people, involving the theft of £250,000. The police believed that SHELLEY, a solicitor, had been passing information to DAWSON about clients and their bank accounts in a conspiracy to commit fraud. DAWSON asked for SHELLEY to represent him while he was in custody. The officer in charge, Detective Chief Inspector PATTERSON, considered making an application to place covert listening devices in the police station interview room, to listen in on their consultation.

Which of the following statements is correct, in relation to the police being allowed to use such surveillance methods?

A This is not permissible, as it amounts to directed surveillance.

B This is permissible, as it only amounts to directed and not intrusive surveillance.

C This is permissible, even though it amounts to intrusive surveillance.

D This is not permissible; all communications between lawyers and their clients are subject to legal privilege.

Question 16.9

PLUNKETT and FERRIS had been arrested by the police for conspiracy to commit murder. They had been interviewed over several days in the police station and neither person made any comment during interview. They were charged with the offence and were being taken to court in the back of a police van. Unknown to the pair, a directed surveillance authority had been obtained to place a covert listening device in the vehicle, which recorded crucial evidence pointing to their guilt.

In relation to the authority obtained, which of the following statements is correct?

A This authority was incorrectly given; this amounted to intrusive surveillance because PLUNKETT and FERRIS were in a vehicle.

B This authority was correctly given; the regulations relating to intrusive surveillance apply only on residential premises.

C This authority was incorrectly given; this amounted to intrusive surveillance because information was obtained using a covert listening device.

D This authority was correctly given; this amounted to directed surveillance because PLUNKETT and FERRIS were not inside a private vehicle.

Question 16.10

The police are investigating an organised crime group suspected of committing a series of armed robberies. Intelligence has been received that key members of the group have arranged to meet in a remote hotel in a week's time. Consideration is being given to applying for an authorisation to conduct surveillance at the hotel with audio and visual devices (microphones and cameras). The investigating officers are planning to place devices in common areas, such as the communal bar and dining room and in private hotel bedrooms.

The Covert Surveillance and Property Interference Code of Practice provides guidance on what is intrusive surveillance. Which of the following is correct in relation to the type of surveillance authorisation the officers would require?

A A directed surveillance authorisation for the common areas and an intrusive surveillance authorisation for the private hotel bedrooms.

B An intrusive surveillance authorisation for the common areas and private hotel bedrooms; a hotel is a 'residential premises' according to the Code.

C A directed surveillance authorisation for the common areas and private hotel bedrooms; a hotel is not a 'residential premises' according to the Code.

D A directed surveillance authorisation for the common areas and an intrusive surveillance authorisation for the private hotel bedrooms; however, if they only plan to use listening devices in the private hotel bedrooms, this would also amount to directed surveillance.

ANSWERS

Answer 16.1

Answer **B** — Article 8 of the European Convention on Human Rights states:

1. Everyone has the right to respect for his private and family life, his home and his correspondence.
2. There shall be no interference by a public authority with the exercise of this right except such as is in accordance with the law and is necessary in a democratic society in the interests of national security, public safety or the economic wellbeing of the country, for the prevention of disorder or crime, for the protection of health or morals, or for the protection of the rights and freedoms of others.

The provisions of Art. 8 extend a right to respect for a person's correspondence (as well as their private life, family life and home). Answer C is therefore incorrect.

Whilst the main aim of the Article is to protect these features of a person's life from arbitrary interference by 'public authorities', the State *does* have a positive obligation to prevent others from interfering with an individual's right to his/her private and family life (*Stjerna* v *Finland* (1994) 24 EHRR 194), and this duty extends beyond simply maintaining public safety. Answers A and D are therefore incorrect.

General Police Duties, para. 4.16.1.1

Answer 16.2

Answer **A** — An offence under s. 1 of the Computer Misuse Act 1990 is committed by causing a computer to perform a function, and all the answers would amount to 'functions'. As you were asked at which point an offence would first be committed, answer A is the correct answer. Although answers B, C and D all may fall under the section, they are incorrect, as switching the computer on is the first function that would amount to the offence.

General Police Duties, para. 4.16.2.1

Answer 16.3

Answer **A** — Under s. 1(1) of the Computer Misuse Act 1990, a person is guilty of an offence if:

(a) he causes a computer to perform any function with intent to secure access to any program or data held in any computer;

(b) the access he intends to secure is unauthorised; and

(c) he knows at the time when he causes the computer to perform the function that that is the case.

In order to prove the offence under s. 1, you must also show that the defendant knew the access was unauthorised and that he/she intended to secure access to the program or data. More proof is required than simply showing the defendant was not authorised to access the data, and therefore answer C is incorrect.

This is an offence of 'specific intent'; therefore, lesser forms of *mens rea* such as recklessness will not be sufficient to convict a person. Answer B is therefore incorrect.

The offence is complete when the person knowingly accesses unauthorised data. There is no requirement to show that he/she knew what the information was being used for (albeit, if BIGNELL *did* know what the data was being used for, she could commit an offence under s. 2 of the Act). Answer D is therefore incorrect.

General Police Duties, para. 4.16.2.1

Answer 16.4

Answer **C** — Under s. 3(1) of the Computer Misuse Act 1990, a person is guilty of an offence if he/she does any unauthorised act in relation to a computer and at the time he/she does the act he/she knows that it is unauthorised; and either subs. (2) or subs. (3) applies.

Under subs. (2), the person must *intend* by doing the act:

(a) to impair the operation of any computer;

(b) to prevent or hinder access to any program or data held in any computer; or

(c) to impair the operation of any such program or the reliability of any such data.

This section is designed to ensure that adequate provision is made to criminalise all forms of denial of service attacks in which the attacker denies the victim(s) access to a particular resource, typically by preventing legitimate users of a service accessing that service. An example of this is where a former employee, acting on a grudge, impaired the operation of a company's computer by using a program to generate and send 5 million emails to the company (*DPP* v *Lennon* [2006] EWHC 1201 (Admin)).

Section 3(3) of the Act states that this subsection also applies if the person is *reckless* as to whether the act will do any of the things mentioned in paras (a) to (c) of subs.

(2) above. Therefore, the offence can be committed by a person who intends or is reckless as to whether the program is impaired and answer B is incorrect.

There is no requirement to prove an intent to cause an economic loss to the company, and therefore answer A is incorrect.

An 'unauthorised act' can include a series of acts, and a reference to impairing, preventing or hindering something includes a reference to doing so temporarily (s. 3(5)), and therefore answer D is incorrect.

General Police Duties, para. 4.16.2.4

Answer 16.5

Answer **B** — The Covert Human Intelligence Sources Code of Practice, Chapter 5, outlines authorisation procedures for the use or conduct of a CHIS. The Code states that on no occasion should the use or conduct of a CHIS under 16 years of age be authorised to give information against his/her *parents or any person who has parental responsibility for him/her*. There is no specific mention of other family members in this Code and answers A, C and D are therefore incorrect.

In other cases involving juvenile CHISs, authorisations should not be granted unless the special provisions contained within the Regulation of Investigatory Powers (Juveniles) Order 2000 (SI 2000/2793) are satisfied.

General Police Duties, para. 4.16.4.4

Answer 16.6

Answer **B** — The Regulation of Investigatory Powers (Directed Surveillance and Covert Human Intelligence Sources) Order 2003 (SI 2003/3171), as amended, sets out the relevant roles and ranks for those who can authorise directed surveillance. In the case of the police the relevant rank will generally be at superintendent level and above, and the authorisation must be in writing except in urgent cases where oral authorisation may be given (s. 43(1)(a)).

Where it is not reasonably practicable to have the application considered by a superintendent or above, having regard to the urgency of the case, then an *inspector may give the relevant authorisation* which will only last 72 hours unless renewed by a superintendent.

Answers A, C and D are therefore incorrect.

General Police Duties, para. 4.16.4.6

Answer 16.7

Answer **C** — If a CHIS authorisation was given orally by a superintendent in an urgent case, it will only last for 72 hours unless renewed. If it is renewed during that time period, it can then last for up to 12 months.

Answers A, B and D are therefore incorrect.

General Police Duties, para. 4.16.4.4

Answer 16.8

Answer **C** — In relation to 'legal privilege' the House of Lords held that the Regulation of Investigatory Powers Act 2000 permits covert surveillance of communications between lawyers and their clients even though these may be covered by legal professional privilege (*Re McE (Northern Ireland)* [2009] UKHL 15). Answers A and D are therefore incorrect.

The Regulation of Investigatory Powers (Extension of Authorisation Provisions: Legal Consultations) Order 2010 (SI 2010/461) provides that directed surveillance carried out in relation to anything taking place on any premises that are being used for the purpose of legal consultations shall be treated as 'intrusive surveillance'. The consultation may be between a professional legal adviser and their client or person representing their client, or with a medical practitioner, where legal proceedings are contemplated and for the purposes of such proceedings.

'Any premises' includes prisons, police stations, legal advisers' business premises and courts. Since the proposal amounts to intrusive surveillance, answers A and B are incorrect.

General Police Duties, para. 4.16.4.6

Answer 16.9

Answer **D** — The Covert Surveillance and Property Interference Code of Practice, Chapter 2, provides guidance on what is intrusive surveillance. Intrusive surveillance is covert surveillance that is carried out in relation to anything taking place on residential premises or in any private vehicle, and that involves the presence of an individual on the premises or in the vehicle or is carried out by a means of a surveillance device. Intrusive surveillance applies to vehicles as well as premises and answer B is incorrect.

In *R v Plunkett* [2013] EWCA Crim 261, in admitting evidence of statements and admissions by the accused in a police van which were covertly recorded, it was held that a police van is not a private vehicle for the purposes of s. 26(3) and that the authorisation given by a superintendent under s. 28 of the Regulation of Investigatory Powers Act 2000 (RIPA) for directed surveillance was appropriate. Answer A is therefore incorrect.

In another case, evidence arising from the use of a bug in police transport, which was obtained in circumstances that meant there was a technical breach of the RIPA authority, was held admissible in that the officers had not acted in bad faith knowing they were exceeding their authority (*Khan* v *R* [2013] EWCA Crim 2230).

The definition of surveillance as intrusive relates to the location of the surveillance, and not any other consideration of the nature of the information that is expected to be obtained (see Code 2.12) or the method of obtaining the information. Answer C is therefore incorrect.

General Police Duties, para. 4.16.4.6

Answer 16.10

Answer **A** — The Covert Surveillance and Property Interference Code of Practice, Chapter 2, provides guidance on what is intrusive surveillance and states:

2.11 Intrusive surveillance is covert surveillance that is carried out in relation to anything taking place on residential premises or in any private vehicle, and that involves the presence of an individual on the premises or in the vehicle or is carried out by means of a surveillance device.

'Residential premises' are considered to be so much of any premises as is for the time being occupied or used by any person, however temporarily, for residential purposes or otherwise as living accommodation. This specifically includes hotel or prison accommodation that is so occupied or used (s. 48(1)). Answer C is therefore incorrect.

However, common areas (such as hotel dining areas) to which a person has access in connection with their use or occupation of accommodation are specifically excluded (s. 48(7)). Answer B is incorrect.

It is irrelevant for these purposes what kind of device the police intend to use to gather evidence; it is either intrusive surveillance according to the guidelines or not. Answer D is therefore incorrect.

General Police Duties, para. 4.16.4.6

17 | Equality

QUESTIONS

Question 17.1

Constable LATTON has approached her sergeant and disclosed that she is considering undergoing gender reassignment surgery. However, she is concerned about discrimination and how the operation would affect her work.

In relation to Constable LATTON's concerns, at what point would she be protected by s. 7(1) of the Equality Act 2010 (protected characteristics of gender reassignment)?

A Constable LATTON would be protected by s. 7 when she has undergone the process and returned to work.

B Constable LATTON would be protected by s. 7 when she has undergone the process, but before she returns to work.

C Constable LATTON would be protected by s. 7 when she is undergoing or has undergone the process.

D Constable LATTON would be protected by s. 7 when she is proposing to undergo, is undergoing or has undergone the process.

Question 17.2

Constable JONES is a response officer and is the sole carer of his elderly parent, who is 94 years of age. Constable JONES has submitted a flexible working request to the senior management team, which would mean working fewer night shifts, but would assist the officer financially due to the cost of carers. The senior management team has rejected the application for operational reasons. Constable JONES is considering taking action against the force for discrimination, citing that the decision of the senior management team is unreasonable.

Which of the following statements would be correct, in relation to constable JONES's potential claim of discrimination?

A Constable JONES would only have to demonstrate that the senior management team's decision was unreasonable, in order to succeed with the claim.

B Constable JONES could succeed with the claim, by showing that some other hypothetical person would have been treated more favourably.

C Constable JONES would have to demonstrate that some other person was treated more favourably, in order to succeed with the claim.

D Constable JONES would have to demonstrate that there would be a tangible or material loss as a result of the decision.

Question 17.3

GRAVETT is a police staff member working in the force Control Room. GRAVETT has been receiving counselling and treatment for depression for a number of years. His GP has recommended a course of medicine which would improve GRAVETT's condition, but would mean that he would need a full night's sleep every night. As a shift worker, this would prove difficult for GRAVETT and he has submitted a request to adjust his shifts to finish at 2 am on night shifts instead of 6 am. The request for reasonable adjustments has been rejected due to operational capacity and GRAVETT has now spoken to a solicitor to discuss a claim of discrimination under the Equality Act 2010.

Which of the following statements would be correct in relation to the level of disadvantage GRAVETT must have suffered, in order for a claim like this to be successful?

A A tribunal would have to conclude that GRAVETT had been placed at a substantial disadvantage by a failure to make reasonable adjustments.

B A tribunal would conclude that even the slightest disadvantage caused to GRAVETT by a failure to make reasonable adjustments would amount to discrimination.

C The threshold for any disadvantage in such a case is that by a failure to make reasonable adjustments, GRAVETT had been caused some disadvantage.

D A tribunal should not have a specific level of disadvantage in mind when deciding whether or not GRAVETT had suffered discrimination; it should make a decision based on the facts presented.

Question 17.4

LEWIN was profoundly deaf and was a suspect in a drug dealing case. Officers executed a warrant at LEWIN's house and found controlled drugs, for which he was arrested. The team had taken Constable SPEARING with them—a Neighbourhood officer, who had had numerous previous dealings with LEWIN and who was confident of being able to communicate the purpose of the search. LEWIN later sued the police for a breach of the Equality Act 2010, on the grounds that they had not provided an interpreter, which put him at a substantial disadvantage during the search.

Which of the following statements is correct, in relation to LEWIN's claim against the police?

A The claim is out of context; if officers have breached the terms of the Police and Criminal Evidence Act 1984, this is an evidential matter and not an equality issue.

B The Equality Act 2010 applies to operational matters; however, there is no disadvantage if the officers and LEWIN were able to communicate without an interpreter.

C The claim is out of context; the Equality Act 2010 does not apply as this is an operational matter and not an employment issue.

D This is a clear breach of the Equality Act 2010 and LEWIN should succeed with his claim against the police.

Question 17.5

Constable GILLIS works as a staff officer to the National Police Chiefs' Council (NPCC) team in her force. The officer is currently on statutory maternity leave, having given birth to her child ten weeks ago. Constable GILLIS had originally stated that she would return to work after 26 weeks (the ordinary maternity leave period), but has now stated that she wishes to take leave for a further 26 weeks (additional maternity leave period). A decision has been taken to move Constable GILLIS to a different post and replace her, because the NPCC team is unable to manage her abstraction for the additional 26 weeks. Constable GILLIS has sought advice from her Federation

Representative, believing that she has been treated unfavourably because of her request for additional maternity leave.

Would Constable GILLIS be protected by s. 18 of the Equality Act 2010, in these circumstances?

A No, s. 18 only applies in the period of 26 weeks after the employee has given birth (ordinary maternity leave period).

B Yes, this is sex discrimination by the employer; Constable GILLIS has been treated less favourably because she is female.

C Yes, Constable GILLIS is in the 'protected period', as defined by s. 18, and has been treated unfavourably.

D No, s. 18 only applies during an employee's pregnancy and two weeks after she has given birth.

Question 17.6

Constable DODD has approached her inspector and disclosed that she believes she is suffering sexual harassment from her sergeant. Constable DODD reported that the sergeant often made remarks about her body in front of other members of the team. In private, he would talk about his sex life and would ask Constable DODD about sexual relationships with her partner. Constable DODD said she had confronted the sergeant about the behaviour and that he had told her that she was imagining the behaviour and that it did not amount to harassment.

What matters should be taken into account in relation to Constable DODD's perception of what had happened during any investigation?

A The investigating officer may take into account Constable DODD's perception of what had happened and compare this to the perception of other members of the team.

B The investigating officer may take into account Constable DODD's perception of what had happened and compare this to the perception of the sergeant.

C The investigating officer must take into account Constable DODD's perception of what had happened, regardless of the perception of other people.

D The investigating officer must take into account Constable DODD's perception of what had happened, depending on the evidence disclosed.

Question 17.7

Constable MELROSE has just started work on a response team in a new area. Officers are aware that before moving to the team, Constable MELROSE had made a complaint of racial discrimination against colleagues on another team and that the complaint had been unsubstantiated. Some officers on Constable MELROSE's new team decided to record problems they encountered with the officer, in fear that they may be the subject of a race discrimination claim at some future date.

Would the officers' behaviour amount to victimisation, because of Constable MELROSE's previous complaint?

A Yes, even though the previous complaint was unsubstantiated, this amounts to victimisation.

B No, if a complaint is unsubstantiated, any future complaint of similar actions cannot amount to victimisation.

C No; however, the officers' behaviour could amount to direct discrimination.

D No, the behaviour of the officers concerned would not amount to victimisation in these circumstances.

Question 17.8

Constable AMIR is suing his police force. The claim relates to a failure by the force to allow Constable AMIR time off to attend a number of religious festivals throughout the year. Constable AMIR's line managers have not been cited as the officer understands the pressures of delivering operational policing; however, the claim is made against the force for failing to have policies and procedures in place to account for the religious beliefs of its staff.

Which of the following statements is correct, in relation to the liability of the police force under s. 42 of the Equality Act 2010?

A Constable AMIR's line managers and the chief constable may be liable; the responsible authority is only liable for discrimination by members of staff towards people outside the force.

B The chief constable alone may be liable in these circumstances; the responsible authority has no liability under this Act.

C The chief constable and the responsible authority may be liable in these circumstances.

D Constable AMIR's line managers may be liable; the chief constable and the responsible authority are only liable for discrimination by members of staff towards people outside the force.

Question 17.9

MARLER has made a claim of discrimination under the Equality Act 2010 against her local police force. MARLER applied for a post as a PCSO and passed what amounted to a national selection process. However, she was told that although she had passed, there were insufficient posts to take her on at this time and that she would be contacted at a later time should any further vacancies arise. However, MARLER has been told by someone working in the recruitment department that the force had appointed three people from black and minority ethnic backgrounds who had also passed the process, but who had scored fewer marks than she had. She had been told this had happened because the force was under-represented in this department by people from black and ethnic minority communities.

Would the behaviour of the force amount to discrimination in employment in these circumstances?

A No, the force can select whom it wants from a pool of people who have passed the process.

B Yes, provided MARLER's performance in the process was better than the people selected ahead of her.

C No, if the force is under-represented by people from black and ethnic minority communities, they can be selected ahead of other candidates provided they passed the process.

D No, provided each candidate was given a fair opportunity to pass the assessment, this is an example of positive action, which the force is entitled to undertake.

Question 17.10

Constable STUBBS is currently suing her employers for discrimination in the workplace. She has cited several instances of inappropriate sexual behaviour towards her by her line managers in work. Constable STUBBS has also included evidence in her statement of inappropriate sexual behaviour towards her by work colleagues while they were at a social Christmas function in a nearby public house.

Would Constable STUBBS be able to rely on *all* of this evidence in her claim of discrimination against her employers?

A Yes, she may be able to rely on this evidence because the function was an extension of the workplace.

B No, but she would have been able to if the behaviour had taken place at an off-duty function at her actual workplace.

C Yes, she may rely on evidence of any inappropriate behaviour, inside or outside the workplace.

D No, her employers cannot be held liable for the behaviour of her colleagues outside the workplace.

ANSWERS

Answer 17.1

Answer **D** — Under s. 7(1) of the Equality Act 2010:

> A person has the protected characteristic of gender reassignment if the person is proposing to undergo, is undergoing or has undergone a process (or part of a process) for the purpose of re-assigning the person's sex by changing physiological or other attributes of sex.

A reference to a transsexual person is a reference to a person who has the protected characteristic of gender reassignment (s. 7(2)).

Since the officer is protected by the Act from the time she is proposing to undergo the operation (effectively now), answers A, B and C are incorrect.

General Police Duties, para. 4.17.3.3

Answer 17.2

Answer **B** — Section 13(1) of the Equality Act 2010 states:

> A person (A) discriminates against another (B) if, because of a protected characteristic, A treats B less favourably than A treats or would treat others.

Less favourable treatment of a person because that person is associated with a protected characteristic, for example because the person has a friend or partner with a particular protected characteristic, or carries out work related to a protected characteristic, is within the scope of this section. This might include carers of disabled people and elderly relatives, who can claim they were treated unfairly because of duties that they had to carry out at home relating to their care work. For example, the non-disabled mother of a disabled child can be discriminated against because of the child's disability (*Coleman* v *Attridge Law* (Case C-303/06) [2008] IRLR 722). This is known as 'associative discrimination'.

To constitute direct discrimination the treatment experienced by B must be different from that of another person. This difference is often referred to as a 'comparator'. The treatment of B must be less favourable than the treatment afforded a comparator. The comparator can be hypothetical where B can establish direct discrimination by showing that if there was another person in similar circumstances, but without B's protected characteristic, that person would be treated more favourably (for an explanation of hypothetical comparators see *Shamoon* v *Chief Constable of the Royal*

Ulster Constabulary [2003] UKHL 11). This is why answer B is correct, and answer C is incorrect.

Less favourable treatment is a broad concept and any disadvantage to which B has been subject will constitute such treatment. B need not have suffered a tangible or material loss (*Chief Constable of West Yorkshire Police* v *Khan* [2001] UKHL 48), and therefore answer D is incorrect.

However, it is not enough merely to show unreasonable treatment (*Bahl* v *The Law Society* [2004] IRLR 799). Answer A is therefore incorrect.

General Police Duties, para. 4.17.4.1

Answer 17.3

Answer **A** — Under s. 20 of the Equality Act 2010, where this Act imposes a duty to make reasonable adjustments, the requirement is that where a provision, criterion or practice puts a disabled person at a *substantial disadvantage* in relation to a relevant matter in comparison with persons who are not disabled, such steps should be taken as it is reasonable to have to take to avoid the disadvantage.

The section contains only one threshold for the reasonable adjustment duty, that of 'substantial disadvantage'; s. 212(1) defines 'substantial' as more than minor or trivial.

Answers B, C and D are therefore incorrect.

General Police Duties, para. 4.17.4.3

Answer 17.4

Answer **B** — Section 13(1) of the Equality Act 2010 states:

A person (A) discriminates against another (B) if, because of a protected characteristic, A treats B less favourably than A treats or would treat others.

Disability is one of the protected characteristics covered by the 2010 Act and the police service has a general 'public sector duty' as a public authority to eliminate discrimination and promote equality (see s. 149).

Section 20 of the Act outlines what is meant by the duty to make reasonable adjustments for the purposes of the Act and, under s. 20(5), the requirement is:

where a disabled person would, but for the provision of an auxiliary aid, be put at a substantial disadvantage in relation to a relevant matter in comparison with persons who are not disabled, to take such steps as it is reasonable to have to take to provide the auxiliary aid.

Section 21 provides that a failure to comply with any one of the reasonable adjustment requirements amounts to discrimination against a disabled person to whom the duty is owed.

The requirement to comply with the 2010 Act applies as much in an operational context as it does in employment legislation; the fact that the officers may have breached PACE is irrelevant in some ways; a discrimination case, if brought about, would be treated as a separate matter and could bring punishment on the force regardless of whether LEWIN is found guilty of supplying drugs. Answers A and C are therefore incorrect.

However, it was held that police officers lawfully searching the home of a man whom they knew to be profoundly deaf did *not* have any effect on the ability of the man and the officers to communicate with each other effectively without a British Sign Language interpreter being present. Officers who had had previous dealings with the man were satisfied on the basis of these dealings that they could achieve a basic level of communication with him without the benefit of an interpreter (*Finnegan* v *Chief Constable of Northumbria* [2013] EWCA Civ 1191). This case demonstrates that the circumstances in the question were not a *clear* breach of the Equality Act 2010 and answer D is therefore incorrect.

General Police Duties, para. 4.17.4.3

Answer 17.5

Answer **C** — An employee generally has the right to 26 weeks of ordinary maternity leave and 26 weeks of additional maternity leave making one year in total. The combined 52 weeks is known as Statutory Maternity Leave.

Section 18 of the Equality Act 2010 states:

(1) This section has effect for the purposes of the application of Part 5 (work) to the protected characteristic of pregnancy and maternity.
(2) A person (A) discriminates against a woman if, in the protected period in relation to a pregnancy of hers, A treats her unfavourably—
   (a) because of the pregnancy, or
   (b) because of illness suffered by her as a result of it.
(3) A person (A) discriminates against a woman if A treats her unfavourably because she is on compulsory maternity leave.
(4) A person (A) discriminates against a woman if A treats her unfavourably because she is exercising or seeking to exercise, or has exercised or sought to exercise, the right to ordinary or *additional* maternity leave.

The duration of the protected period depends on the statutory maternity leave entitlements as set out in the Employment Rights Act 1996, which defines the right to compulsory, ordinary and additional maternity leave. The protected period starts when a woman becomes pregnant and ends either:

- if she has the right to ordinary and additional maternity leave, at the end of the additional maternity leave period or (if earlier) when she returns to work after the pregnancy; or
- if she does not have that right, at the end of the period of two weeks beginning with the end of the pregnancy.

Answer A is incorrect, because compulsory maternity leave is only one of the areas covered by s. 18.

Answer D is incorrect since the officer has a statutory entitlement to ordinary and additional maternity leave; the protection does not end two weeks after she has given birth, it ends when she returns to work.

Whilst this case may amount to a breach of s. 18, sex discrimination does not apply to treatment of a woman insofar as it is in the protected period, or it is for a reason mentioned in s. 18(3) or (4). Answer B is therefore incorrect.

General Police Duties, para. 4.17.4.6

Answer 17.6

Answer **C** — Under s. 26 of the Equality Act 2010:

(1) A person (A) harasses another (B) if—
  (a) A engages in unwanted conduct related to a relevant protected characteristic, and
  (b) the conduct has the purpose or effect of—
    (i) violating B's dignity, or
    (ii) creating an intimidating, hostile, degrading, humiliating or offensive environment for B.
(2) A also harasses B if—
  (a) A engages in unwanted conduct of a sexual nature, and
  (b) the conduct has the purpose or effect referred to in subsection (1)(b).

The behaviour referred to involves unwanted conduct which is related to a relevant characteristic and has the purpose or effect of creating an intimidating, hostile, degrading, humiliating or offensive environment for the complainant or of violating the complainant's dignity (which is described clearly in this question).

In deciding whether conduct has the effect referred to in s. 26(1)(b), the perception of B, the other circumstances of the case, and whether it is reasonable for the conduct to have that effect, must be taken into account (s. 26(4)).

Therefore, while the investigating officer *may* take into account the perception of other members of the team weighing up the evidence against the sergeant, he or she must take into account the victim's perception of what happened.

Answers A, B and D are therefore incorrect.

General Police Duties, para. 4.17.4.8

Answer 17.7

Answer **D** — Section 27 of the Equality Act 2010 states:

(1) A person (A) victimises another person (B) if A subjects B to a detriment because—
  (a) B does a protected act, or
  (b) A believes that B has done, or may do, a protected act.
(2) Each of the following is a protected act—
  (a) bringing proceedings under this Act;
  (b) giving evidence or information in connection with proceedings under this Act;
  (c) doing any other thing for the purposes of or in connection with this Act;
  (d) making an allegation (whether or not express) that A or another person has contravened this Act.

This would mean that generally, if a person makes a claim, he/she could still be the subject of victimisation at some time in the future, regardless of whether the claim was substantiated. Answer B is therefore incorrect.

However, in *Bayode* v *Chief Constable of Derbyshire* [2008] UKEAT 0499 07 2205, the tribunal held that the complainant, a police constable who was a black African and Nigerian by national origin, had *not* been victimised where his colleagues recorded any problems they encountered with him in their PNBs for fear that he might make a race discrimination claim at some future date. Previous unsubstantiated discrimination claims had been made by the complainant. Answer A is therefore incorrect.

Direct discrimination is an entirely different matter to victimisation, and generally involves employers treating one group of people less favourably than others based on protected grounds, such as their racial origin, marital status, sex, religion or belief or sexual orientation. It is out of context in this scenario, and for that reason answer C is incorrect.

General Police Duties, para. 4.17.4.10

Answer 17.8

Answer **C** — Section 42 of the Equality Act 2010 states:

(1) For the purposes of this Part, holding the office of constable is to be treated as employment—
   (a) by the chief officer, in respect of any act done by the chief officer in relation to a constable or appointment to the office of constable;
   (b) by the responsible authority, in respect of any act done by the authority in relation to a constable or appointment to the office of constable.

The Equality Act 2010 makes provisions for chief officers *and* 'responsible' authorities to be liable for acts done by them towards their staff. Answer B is therefore incorrect.

This liability is not limited to discrimination by members of staff towards people outside the force; it can include discrimination by members of staff towards people within the force, and therefore answers A and D are incorrect.

The chief officer of police is also vicariously liable for acts of race discrimination by staff under his/her direction and control. The statutory defence that an employer took all reasonable steps to prevent the acts of discrimination complained of is also available to chief officers (s. 109(4)).

General Police Duties, paras 4.17.5, 4.17.7

Answer 17.9

Answer **B** — Under s. 39 of the Equality Act 2010, it is unlawful for an employer to discriminate against or victimise employees and people seeking work. It applies where the employer is making arrangements to fill a job, and in respect of anything done in the course of a person's employment.

There are a number of exceptions and defences to the provisions of the Act, but two of the more relevant defences in relation to discrimination or victimisation in employment are 'genuine occupational requirement' and 'positive action'.

'Positive action' refers to measures to alleviate disadvantage experienced by people who share a protected characteristic, reduce their under-representation in relation to particular activities and meet their particular needs (s. 158). It allows for measures to be targeted to particular groups, including training to enable them to gain employment, but any such measures must be a proportionate way of achieving the relevant aim.

An employer may also take a protected characteristic into consideration when deciding whom to recruit or promote, where people having the protected characteristic are at a disadvantage or are under-represented (s. 159).

However, this can be done only where the candidates are as qualified as each other. Therefore, if the three people with black or minority ethnic backgrounds had scored the same as MARLER in the assessment centre, the force has used positive action correctly, but if they had scored fewer marks, the force has not. The aim is to help employers achieve a more diverse workforce by giving them the option, when faced with candidates of *equal merit*, to choose a candidate from an under-represented group.

Answers A, C and D are therefore incorrect.

General Police Duties, para. 4.17.6

Answer 17.10

Answer **A** — Section 109 of the Equality Act 2010 states:

(1) Anything done by a person (A) in the course of A's employment must be treated as also done by the employer.

(2) ...

(3) It does not matter whether that thing is done with the employer's or principal's knowledge or approval.

Where acts amounting to discrimination take place outside the workplace, the employer and employees may still be caught within the framework of the legislation. So, for instance, where police officers engage in inappropriate sexual behaviour towards a colleague at a work-related social function, a tribunal may be entitled to hold that the function was an extension of the workplace and so hold the chief officer liable for the acts of his/her officers at that function (*Chief Constable of Lincolnshire* v *Stubbs* [1999] IRLR 81). Answer D is therefore incorrect.

This case deals with a specific example of behaviour where the officers were at a work-related function, which was an 'extension of the workplace'. The decision does not, therefore, mean that any behaviour can be included in such a claim (although it is worth noting that discrimination and victimisation are included in the Code of Conduct for police officers, which may include the conduct of an off-duty officer). Answer C is therefore incorrect. Lastly, this case did not specify that the location of the function was important, merely that it was an off-duty function and an extension of the workplace. Answer B is therefore incorrect.

General Police Duties, para. 4.17.7

Question Checklist

The following checklist is designed to help you keep track of your progress when answering the multiple-choice questions. If you fill this in after one attempt at each question, you will be able to check how many you have got right and which questions you need to revisit a second time. Also available online; to download visit www.blackstonespoliceservice.com.

	First attempt Correct (✓)	Second attempt Correct (✓)
1 Complaints and Misconduct		
1.1		
1.2		
1.3		
1.4		
1.5		
1.6		
1.7		
1.8		
1.9		
1.10		
1.11		
2 Unsatisfactory Performance and Attendance		
2.1		
2.2		
2.3		
2.4		

	First attempt Correct (✓)	Second attempt Correct (✓)
2.5		
2.6		
2.7		
2.8		
2.9		
2.10		
3 Stop and Search		
3.1		
3.2		
3.3		
3.4		
3.5		
3.6		
3.7		
3.8		
3.9		
3.10		
3.11		

	First attempt Correct (✓)	Second attempt Correct (✓)
3.12		
3.13		
3.14		
3.15		
3.16		
3.17		
4 Entry, Search and Seizure		
4.1		
4.2		
4.3		
4.4		
4.5		
4.6		
4.7		
4.8		
4.9		
4.10		
4.11		
4.12		
5 Powers of Arrest		
5.1		
5.2		
5.3		
5.4		
5.5		
5.6		
5.7		
5.8		

	First attempt Correct (✓)	Second attempt Correct (✓)
5.9		
5.10		
5.11		
5.12		
5.13		
6 Hatred and Harassment Offences		
6.1		
6.2		
6.3		
6.4		
6.5		
6.6		
6.7		
6.8		
6.9		
6.10		
6.11		
6.12		
7 Anti-social Behaviour		
7.1		
7.2		
7.3		
7.4		
7.5		
7.6		
7.7		
7.8		
7.9		
7.10		

	First attempt Correct (✓)	Second attempt Correct (✓)
7.11		
7.12		

8 Offences Involving Communications

	First attempt Correct (✓)	Second attempt Correct (✓)
8.1		
8.2		
8.3		
8.4		
8.5		
8.6		
8.7		
8.8		
8.9		
8.10		

9 Terrorism and Associated Offences

	First attempt Correct (✓)	Second attempt Correct (✓)
9.1		
9.2		
9.3		
9.4		
9.5		
9.6		
9.7		
9.8		

10 Public Order, Processions and Assemblies

	First attempt Correct (✓)	Second attempt Correct (✓)
10.1		
10.2		
10.3		
10.4		
10.5		
10.6		
10.7		
10.8		
10.9		
10.10		
10.11		
10.12		
10.13		
10.14		
10.15		
10.16		
10.17		
10.18		

11 Sporting Events

	First attempt Correct (✓)	Second attempt Correct (✓)
11.1		
11.2		
11.3		
11.4		
11.5		

12 Weapons

	First attempt Correct (✓)	Second attempt Correct (✓)
12.1		
12.2		
12.3		
12.4		
12.5		
12.6		
12.7		
12.8		
12.9		

	First attempt Correct (✓)	Second attempt Correct (✓)
12.10		
12.11		
12.12		

13 Protection of People Suffering from Mental Disorders

	First attempt Correct (✓)	Second attempt Correct (✓)
13.1		
13.2		
13.3		

14 Offences Relating to Land and Premises

	First attempt Correct (✓)	Second attempt Correct (✓)
14.1		
14.2		
14.3		
14.4		
14.5		

15 Licensing and Offences Relating to Alcohol

	First attempt Correct (✓)	Second attempt Correct (✓)
15.1		
15.2		
15.3		
15.4		
15.5		
15.6		
15.7		
15.8		
15.9		
15.10		

	First attempt Correct (✓)	Second attempt Correct (✓)
15.11		
15.12		
15.13		

16 Offences and Powers Relating to Information

	First attempt Correct (✓)	Second attempt Correct (✓)
16.1		
16.2		
16.3		
16.4		
16.5		
16.6		
16.7		
16.8		
16.9		
16.10		

17 Equality

	First attempt Correct (✓)	Second attempt Correct (✓)
17.1		
17.2		
17.3		
17.4		
17.5		
17.6		
17.7		
17.8		
17.9		
17.10